A FOOTING ON THIS EARTH

By Sara Henderson Hay

A FOOTING ON THIS EARTH

STORY HOUR

THE STONE AND THE SHELL
(*Pegasus Award*)

THE DELICATE BALANCE
(*Edna St. Vincent Millay Memorial Award*)

THIS, MY LETTER

FIELD OF HONOR
(*Kaleidograph Award*)

A FOOTING
ON THIS EARTH

Sara Henderson Hay

1966

DOUBLEDAY & COMPANY, INC., GARDEN CITY, NEW YORK

To my mother, and to the memory of my father

Poems in this book have appeared in the following periodicals: *Voices, Commonweal, The New York American, The New York Times, The New York Herald Tribune, The Christian Century, Harper's Bazaar, Scribner's Magazine, Forum, Good Housekeeping, Canadian Bookman, Kaleidograph Magazine, Bozart, The Miraculous Medal, Harper's Magazine, Poetry World, The Christian Science Monitor, Ladies' Home Journal, Literary Digest, Atlantic Monthly, Psychology, The Saturday Review of Literature, American Poetry Journal, The American Girl, Hygeia, The New York Sun, North American Review, Columbia, McCall's, Show, The Lyric, Scholastic, The Classmate, Yankee,* and the following poems appeared originally in *The New Yorker*: ON FINDING A SNAKE, WITH ITS HEAD CRUSHED; THE SNAIL; SONG BEFORE SPRING; THE PESSIMIST; PIGEON ENGLISH; TO AN OLD WOMAN ON THE SUBWAY; GRASSHOPPER IN THE CEMETERY; TO MY SMALL SON, BUSY IN THE BACK YARD; TO MY SMALL SON, IN CHURCH; TO MY SMALL SON, ROLLER-SKATING; TO MY SMALL SON, ON CERTAIN OCCASIONS; THE CURLEW; TIDAL POOL; NATURAL HISTORY NOTE; THE SURVIVOR.

TABLE OF CONTENTS

Dedication for a Book   xvii

TIMES AND SEASONS   1

April   3
Song before Spring   4
She Contemplates Death   5
For a Premature Spring   6
For a Poplar, in a City Court   7
Midsummer   8
In the Cool of the Evening . . .   9
Frost . . . First Casualties   10
Fog at Morning   11
Racing the Rain   12
On Turning Over a Stone   13
The Daily Manna   14
The Deeper Wisdom   15

INNER WEATHER   17

From the Sunset   19
The Warnings   20
Conversation à Deux   21
The Riddle   22
Heresy Indeed . . .   23
Philosophy   24
Mount Monadnock, from My Studio   25
The Challenge   26
The Shell   27

Visitant   28
Night Thought   29
Trick of Memory   30
Of Faith   31
Bottle Should Be Plainly Labeled "Poison"   32
Unequal Conflict   33
Ledge Above Water   34
Reassurance   35
The Incompleat Nature Lover   36
Revenge   37
The Examples   38
On Suicide   39
On Being Too Inhibited   39
Analysis   40
Foreboding   41
Some Wealth More Sure   42
The Cry   43
The Lie   44
For Pot-boiling   45
The Perverse Poet   46
Tiller of Soil   47
The Poet   47
Assurance   48
The Change   49
Beginner   50

SEASONS OF THE HEART   51
Problem   53
Unsophisticate   54
Tell Me, Gypsy . . .   55
Concerning Cupid   56
For a Misunderstanding, Settled upon the Spot   57
To One Who Overlooks My Faults   58
After Quarreling   59
Requiem   60
Object Lesson   61

Out of the Blue   61
Well Lost for Love   62
No Phantom   63
Field of Honor I, II, III   64
On the Perspective of Grief   66
The Silent Ones   67
A Long Time After   68
Advice to a Lady   69
Advice to a Gentleman   70
The Propitiator   71
Thanksgiving   72
3 A.M.   73
Bright Face of Danger   74
Premonition   75
The Wind   76
The Winter Reason   77
Explanation   78
Natural History Note   79
The Hoax   80
The Death   81
The Wound   82
The Survivor   83
The Difference   84

MEN AND WOMEN   85
Portrait of a Certain Gentleman   87
Portrait of a Selfish Man   88
For a Certain Kindly Atheist   89
Of Certain Righteous   90
Church Funeral for a Certain Gentleman   91
Object Lesson for a Certain Gentleman   92
Portrait from Nature   92
The Man Who Took Literally the Advice of Three Monkeys   93
Destiny   94
The Man Who Loved Care   95
Portrait of a Certain Lady   96

Portrait of a Lady   97
For a Spinster, Dying of Cancer of the Breast   98
Problem for the Psychiatrist   99
To an Old Woman on the Subway   100
Public Figure   101
The Prudent Man   102
Ogre's Castle   103
Observation   104
Counsel   105
Ed Jones 1933   Bill Smith 1936   Jim Turner 1928   106
The Man Named Legion   107
On Contemplating an Open Fire   108
Salute to Man   109
Ex Tenebris   110
    I   Ex Tenebris
    II What the Medium Said
Hic Jacet   111
    I   Epitaph for a Certain Gentleman
    II Epitaph for a Certain Lady
    III Epitaph for a Little Grave
Grasshopper in the Cemetery   112
Epitaph for a Spinster   113
Boy in the Woods   114
To My Small Son, Busy in the Back Yard   115
To My Small Son, in Church   116
To My Small Son, Beach-combing   117
To My Small Son, Roller-skating   118
To My Small Son, on Certain Occasions   119
To My Small Son, Growing Up   120

ANOTHER STORY   121

Dedication   123
The Builders   124
Syndicated Column   125
Dr. S— Interviews a Worried Mother   126
Local Boy Makes Good   127

The Sleeper I, II   128
The Investigator   130
I Remember Mama   131
The Princess   132
Only Son   133
Welfare Report   134
The Witch   135

BIRDS AND BEASTS   137

The Curlew   139
Pigeon English   140
For a Little Bird that Blundered into Church   141
The Pessimist   142
For a Locust that Died, Emerging from Its Chrysalis   143
For a Praying Mantis, on a City Street   144
The Snail   145
Little Fable   146
For a Dead Kitten   147
The Monkey   148
Words for a Young Wild Thing   149
Tidal Pool   150
On Finding a Snake, with Its Head Crushed   151
Incident in Gethsemane   152
In the Garden   153
    I   The Lizard
    II Local Bethesda
    III ". . . Wars, and rumors of wars. . . ."
    IV Under the Arbor
Sanctuary   156
The Beasts   157
Incident with Lions   158
The Beasts at Judgment   159

"SURELY I WOULD SPEAK TO THE ALMIGHTY,
    AND I DESIRE TO REASON WITH GOD."   161

On Contemplating an Honest, Rosy-cheeked Apple   163

One Hesitant   164
Text   165
The Fire   166
The Favored   167
These Hands   168
Accusation   169
In Flood and Dearth   170
Jacob Sings   171
The Happy Land   172
The Fight   173
"As it was in the beginning . . ."   174

WITNESS FOR THE DEFENSE   175

Witness for the Defense   177
Eden I, II, III, IV, V   178
Sic Transit   183
The Prodigal   184
The Father   184
The Elder Son   185
For Lot's Wife   186
Delilah   187
Behold this Dreamer   188
The Nightmare   189
Noah   190
The Return   192

SWEET STORY OF OLD   193

Joseph to Mary   195
Mary to Joseph   196
When Mary Was a Little Maid   197
The Gifts   198
Christmas the Year One, A.D.   199
Mary   200
In Nazareth   201
The Child   202
In the Servants' Hall   203

Night of Calvary   204
The Neighbors   206
Ballad of the Golden Bowl   208

THE SEARCH   211

Ultimate Valor   213
The Search   214
De Profundis   215
Defense   216
Beside the Brook   217
Prayer to Mary   218
"Not made with hands . . ."   219
"Therefore with Angels and Archangels . . ."   220

DEDICATION FOR A BOOK

I shall not lose a footing on this earth
So long as any song of mine remain;
Essential substance of my heart and brain,
The valuation of my honest worth.
More of my self will move in word and line
Than ever walked abroad in flesh and bone—
Herein am I most intimately known,
Whoever reads may be a friend of mine.

He shall perceive that I was gay, and candid,
And not too trustful in my heart's behalf;
That I was obstinate, and open-handed,
And held no grudges, and was quick to laugh;
That, clinging stubbornly to hope and breath,
I had no enmity at all for Death.

TIMES AND SEASONS

APRIL

Spring comes with ordered, geometric precision.
There is no uncertainty about grass.
April is always observing the nice division
Of leaf and bud and bloom; no day can pass
Without its quota of jonquils. Flowers are
Products of an exact measurement; one perceives
The beautiful, balanced angles of a star.
There are no incongruities in leaves.
Even the rain falls
In silver verticals.

SONG BEFORE SPRING

What word informs the pear?
What syllable persuades
The jonquil's pointed blades
To thrust against the air?

It is still cold. The day
Wakens to frosty light.
Frost ushers in the night.
In what most subtle way

Does the news reach the root
Under the chilly ground?
Some sound that is not sound
Quickens the alder shoot.

Sap tingles like the blood.
Touch the bough, cold in sleep,
And feel the swift pulse leap
Warm in the living wood.

SHE CONTEMPLATES DEATH

"I shall not mind at all," she said,
"The comfortable earth will make
A welcome and a gracious bed,
As fine a couch as one could ask.
It will be pleasant, being dead,
At drowsy intervals to wake
And know the small grass, overhead,
Is at its green, perennial task.
When one so quietly has lain
How excellent to hear the sound
Of delicately fallen rain,
And in the quickened earth around
To feel the glad roots, underground,
Busy with April once again!"

FOR A PREMATURE SPRING

So prescient of grief
At this untimely birth,
Had you no warning, earth,
For the confiding leaf?

For the so-trustful shoot,
The unsuspicious grass?
Was there no way, alas,
To hold the struggling root?

To quell the eager blood
In every sapling's vein,
To fold the flower again,
To furl the valiant bud?

Were they of such small worth,
Tendril, and leaf, and bloom?
Reading their frosty doom,
You might have warned them, earth!

FOR A POPLAR, IN A CITY COURT

I had forgotten that the world
Wore such a shining grace of green,
Or that a poplar tip, unfurled,
Could bow upon the wind, and lean
So delicately on the air—
The same thin tree that, winter long,
Stood desolate and stripped and spare.
I did not know that it was strong
As gentle things can often be
To come into its own again,
Or could so tacitly make plain
All the loud winter hid from me.

MIDSUMMER

"A hot summer makes a bright fall . . ."
PROVERB

A dusty bee fumbles among the roses;
He shoves the petals aside and crawls, complaining,
Into the tilted room, and sprawls, and dozes.
The garden is sick with summer, worn with straining
After its failing breath; the weary grass
Shrinks from the quivering rocks, the leaves are curled
Limp on the stricken fern, and the sky is glass
Blown to a monstrous bubble above the world.

Even the locust, whom sultry days embolden
To crack the silence with a skirling tune
Winds feebly down, his lusty voice is jaded.
The wastrel sun strides on. I am persuaded
Autumn will meet, in scarlet leaf and golden,
The obligation of this afternoon.

8

IN THE COOL OF THE EVENING ...

The day, the golden light, is gone,
And quietly the evening drifts
Over the land. Now the young moon
Leading the first star heavenward, lifts
Her slender lantern in the sky,
And shadow, like a dappled fawn,
Steps delicately forth to try
The pool of silver on the lawn.

Oh do not speak—this is the hour
For crickets in the garden wall,
For drowsy bird and folded flower.
This is that half-light interval
Serene and beautiful, as though
God lifted up a gentle hand
For silence, that His world might know
He walks at evening through the land.

FROST ... FIRST CASUALTIES

Here failed the bright, industrious wing,
The bee who toiled through the brave spring,
Knew summer as heaped flower on flower,
How fell she on this bitter hour?

And the slow worm, caught out-of-ground
In all his supple misery, found
An alien cold, immense, unknown,
Twisted, and stiffened on the stone.

FOG AT MORNING

The fog, imponderable, vast,
Smothered a startled world, and cowed
Meadow and little road, aghast
At the chill presence of the cloud.

And when the evil thing had wreathed
Its slow way upward, and was gone,
How thankfully the scared earth breathed,
And swore the sun had never shone

With so incredible a grace,
Or worn so well-beloved a face!

RACING THE RAIN

As though there leapt within his brain
The strong-limbed fox that tempts the chase,
Ecstatic terror sets his pace
Who runs, who runs before the rain . . .

Who feels the strange excitement flood
His pricking senses through and through,
And times his ardent muscles to
A lovely panic of his blood—

But almost fears to look behind
Lest somewhere, somehow, he should spy
Along the margin of the sky
A lean hound snuffing up the wind.

ON TURNING OVER A STONE

In the grass, in the ditch, at the feet of childhood it lay,
Angular, bulky, adamant—a boulder
Half buried in the turf, thrusting its shoulder
Out of the ground. Do you remember the day
We rolled it over, and what we found beneath:
A strange, flat universe, an alien world
That scuttled in glossy armor, or slow uncurled,
While we knelt in the grass on our knees, and held our breath?

And that was long ago—and I did not say
"What will people think, that I pause for wonder
In a ditch, beside a shifted pebble? Or stoop
To a jointed, crystal-eyed creature?" This latter day
I am too proud, too wise. I am too grown-up
To turn a stone and discover a world thereunder.

THE DAILY MANNA

". . . there is nothing at all, beside this manna!"
Complaint of the Children of Israel.
NUMBERS 11: 6

If suddenly, wonderfully, glittering among the leaves
The fabled, the gilded Phoenix would break from cover!
But here is only a small, brown-breasted bird that grieves
In a few plaintive notes at dusk, over and over.

Oh, if a milk-white Unicorn would appear,
And stamp with silvery hooves at the edge of the meadow!
But that which moves near the birches is only a deer
Dappled with light and shadow.

I wish I could take three steps into an enchanted wood.
But *this* is only the grove where the lovers come,
At evening, the whispering boys and girls; only the valley road,
The long way home.

THE DEEPER WISDOM

How should I, city born and bred,
With all my being understand
That word the meadow softly said,
The speaking silence of the land,

Except that, to my inmost bone,
There came assurance, sharp and true,
Of something man has always known
But not remembered that he knew:

The versatile, the veering mind
Loves many things that shift and change,
And to no form or state aligned
Goes after foreign gods and strange.

Not so the humble flesh and blood
Which dies—and knowing it must die,
Looks on this field and blowing wood
With deeper wisdom in its eye,

And finds in simple earth and stone
A permanence to make its own.

INNER WEATHER

FROM THE SUNSET

"Death rides from the sunset . . ."
OLD SPANISH PROVERB

This is a city walled secure,
Foursquare to foe and bitter weather,
And three inhabitants there are,
Dwelling in amity together.

At the south gate the gentle heart
Has taken lodging of her own,
A quiet garden, fixed apart,
And for love's entering alone.

Upon the north the studious mind
Sets up a guild, and finds it good.
He welcomes others of his kind,
A strict, polemic brotherhood.

Eastward, the contemplative soul
Has built a shrine, in peace and prayer.
Remote and unassailable
She meditates unsistered there.

But all the three keep watch upon
The close-barred gateway to the west,
Knowing that it must swing to one
Most certain and impartial guest.

THE WARNINGS

How clear in the reflective mind
The portents of disaster stand,
After the fact, and late, alas:
The snake's dry whisper in the grass,
The sixth wave high at the tide's edge,
In the gray skies an arrowy wedge,
The wrinkled leaf on the green branch,
The evening earlier on the land,
The pebble skittering down the sand
Before the impending avalanche.

CONVERSATION A DEUX

This fact is borne upon me plain:
We cannot meet and talk, my friend,
As strict identities, as twain
Who speak their minds, and comprehend.
Not I to you, or you to me
As two—but three confronting three.

I am that self I wish to show,
(Which is the natural, human sham),
I am, as well, that self you know.
And last, the self I really am.
So, intricately joined, the three
Compose my triple entity.

And you are no wise different.
For every soul beneath the sun
Is similarly fused and blent,
Three personalities, not one.
Two may not meet as simple two,
However they might wish it true. . . .

THE RIDDLE

I am as one who has a starving anger,
A metaphysical want in his soul's middle.
And yet what food will satisfy that hunger
Remains my stubborn riddle.

Because, for some inexplicable reason,
I have preferred perversely to deny
That I was hungry; I have practiced treason
To lay the anguish by.

My troubled soul I caution: "Do not taste.
Nausea is worse than any hunger felt."
I am as one who swears he will subsist
By tightening up his belt.

Unless I go about to mend my ways,
The creature, famishing, will forfeit breath.
I may discover, one of these fine days,
That I have starved to death.

HERESY INDEED . . .

"Therefore a health to all that shot and missed!"
THE TAMING OF THE SHREW

It is a piteous thing to be
Enlisted in no cause at all,
Unsworn to any heraldry,
To fly no banner from the wall,
Own nothing you would sweat or try for,
Or bruise your hands or bleed or die for.

This were a greater sin against
That hostage of your living breast,
Than to rouse all the world incensed
At something you believed your quest,
And stormed the skies and suffered pain for,
And fell and cursed and fought again for.

To take the smooth and middle path,
The half-heart interest, the creed
Without extreme of hope or wrath,
Ah, this were heresy indeed
That all God's pity will not stay for,
And your immortal soul will pay for!

PHILOSOPHY

To sow, but reckon for a tardy spring;
To hoard, keeping in mind the moth and rust;
To dream, but not confuse the wakening;
To smile, and guard against the foeman's thrust.
To hope, but put no credence in the thing,
Beyond its possibility; to trust,
But never blindly so, considering
The prescient and meditative dust.

MOUNT MONADNOCK, FROM MY STUDIO

If I had faith enough, I could
Move that old mountain, which has stood
Immutable upon its base
More centuries than I've had days.

What I could do, if I had faith—
The thought's enough to take my breath!
I wonder if the mountain sees
My vast potentialities.

It need not fear me, from its height
Of cloudy dappled dark and light;
Still stand, unshaken, solid, sound,
The lesser hills that hem me round.

THE CHALLENGE

No larger reason of the mind
Could urge me out of body and bone;
Not curiosity alone
For what the soul might find;

Nor any questing after peace
Beyond tumultuous dark and light;
Not tears, nor wide-eyed thought at night,
I have no quarrel with these.

I never scorned the pleasant breath,
But the sheer knowledge that I *could*,
At will, have done with flesh and blood,
Draws me to think on death.

Tremendous challenge in the fact
That half a minute, and a knife,
Are all one needs to close a life.
Even that simpler act

Of leaning farther than a sill,
Or certain pellets neatly downed.
A trigger-finger, crooked around
Just so—is easier still.

It is the technique of the art
Enchants me past the narrow fears
Of silence crowding on the ears
And stricture at the heart.

THE SHELL

Not memory of the heart's dark treasons
Wrung out of terror or need or pride,
Nothing recalled to my dishonor
Shapes the smooth house where I reside.

Not what in pity I *remember*
Rounds my snug roof and keeps it mended—
By all I have with care forgotten
I am most durably defended.

VISITANT

The waters of the mind are cool
And filled with stars at starry eve;
Bethesda, with a quiet spring
Deep at its silver source—and yet
Holding no healing for the soul
Which in her sore distress must grieve
Until, with downward shattering wing,
Some grave-eyed angel trouble it.

NIGHT THOUGHT

The brain works smoothest in the night,
That clever instrument is geared
To subtler ratios than light;
So intricately engineered

That not a tremor will attest
The tissues' strain; nor is there found
A whisper past the narrow breast,
Above the muffled heart a sound.

TRICK OF MEMORY

Sometimes the effort to recall a fact
Approaches almost the sheer physical act
Of looking at something beyond the eye's range,
And having its outlines waver and blur and change,
Unfocused in the direct, forward stare.
It may, however, be taken unaware
By the eye's simple and expedient trick
Of looking at it, then looking away, then quick
Looking again, and seeing it plain, before
The vision falters and the shape's obscure.
The fact forgotten stands indistinct, and plays
Thus with the tense mind's astigmatic gaze.
But think on it. Then think away. After unnumbered
Trials you may suddenly catch it clear, remembered!

OF FAITH

The structure of my faith is such
I cannot say "Lo, there it stands."
Dissolving backwards at my touch,
It slips my stare, eludes my hands.
Yet from the corner of my eye
I see it towering straight and high,
And know it definite as sky.

BOTTLE SHOULD BE PLAINLY LABELED "POISON"

Too powerful a drug is Hope
For constant use, and every day.
It warps the present's able scope,
It leads the wishful wits astray.

That eye which Hope has focused far
Upon some visionary good,
Is blinded by a distant star
To the small flowers of the wood.

Man builds of simple stones a palace,
The dry plain, tended, greens with grass.
Who looks the most to future solace
Will make the least of what he has.

There is a delicate balance set
Between Hope's virtue and its vice.
The man who takes it to forget,
Must know how little will suffice.

UNEQUAL CONFLICT

Hardship is honest, and a foe
That a brave man may overthrow
In open battle, hand to hand.
A man may challenge him, and stand.
Strife and assault can never best
The beating heart within man's breast,
But ambuscade and treacheries
Bring him outnumbered to his knees.
Injustice is the heathen lord
Who wields a double-edgèd sword,
Who knows the conqueror's final art
Of setting heel upon that heart.

LEDGE ABOVE WATER

I never felt him quite so near before,
The visible shape of death,
As in that water heaving to the shore
Its huge and sullen breath.

The slow wave coiled its muscled strength, and swerved
Against the ledge in thunder,
Doubled upon itself, rose up, and curved
A hollow cavern under

Whereto had I been bold enough to lean
In that brief moment's space,
I had beheld one better left unseen,
Had looked upon death's face.

And not, I think, the pictured-as-a-skull,
Nor in the charmed sight blurred,
But sharp and venomous and beautiful
A serpent to a bird.

The mocking mouth, the glittering cold gaze,
The dark hair swept oblique—
I could have leaned until his hand might raise
To touch my cheek,

Except that flooding panic made me rise
And flee the peril then
For fear that I should stare into death's eyes
Nor look away again.

REASSURANCE

I heard a pebble say
"I prop this canyon wall.
If I should once give way
The mountainside would fall."
He said "It's lucky for *you*
I keep my stubborn place."
And looking at his stern face
I half believed it true!

THE INCOMPLEAT NATURE LOVER

Stiff in my tracks, so not to scare
The clover-cropping deer,
I stand until I creak; on my cramped knee
Wait for the squirrel to spiral down the tree.

Blue-knuckled in the cold, I strew
Largesse upon the snow,
And with munificence of seed and crumb
Entreat the birds to come.

With what forbearance I endure
The cat's supreme hauteur;
Affronted thrice, I turn the other cheek.
I bark myself, to teach my dog to speak.

Yet can, alas, for my own kind
So small a portion find
Of the enormous patience I expend
To make a bird, or little beast, my friend.

REVENGE

I wandered down into a grove
And sat beneath a tree,
When from the branches up above,
An insect spat at me.

Only a tiny dewy drop,
Yet furious I grew
To think that any creature did
What that had dared to do.

I straightway ran and seized an axe
Beside my cottage door
And smote the sapling root and branch
Till hands and back were sore.

"This is the only way," I said
"My wound to rectify."
Therefore (the insect having flown)
I left the tree to die.

THE EXAMPLES

The spider at her task,
The ant, the burdened bee,
No one's appraisal ask,
They know what they must do;
And all the summer's day pursue
Their single-minded industry.

The oak beside my door,
The moss upon the stone,
Do not, I think, require
Counsel from anyone,
Or shape themselves to grow, or be,
Other than candid moss and tree.

Whom do I seek to please?
Whose censure would avoid
That with such strategies
I am so much employed?
All things I spend myself upon
Except my true vocation.

I wish I could put forth
My leaves, or spin my tents,
Or burrow in my earth
With such fine confidence
In my own purposes; could be
Sufficient, unperplexed, as they.

ON SUICIDE

With this concise equation may be solved
A sum or two of fate;
This trick of flesh which is not *too* involved,
Nor very intricate,

And, save a certain conquerable fear,
Easily done.
So neighborly is death, so strangely near
Oblivion.

ON BEING TOO INHIBITED

Now may the pitying eye discern
The pinched and wistful soul
Of one who was so late to learn
That often "self-control"

Is neither more nor less, in truth,
Than just the meager art
Of planing the emotions smooth
And chiseling the heart.

ANALYSIS

Because it stretched my breast apart
I held in check my growing heart;
Because I feared a curbless mind
Might leave my ordered ways behind,
I took no chances with the steed.
But finding that I had a need
To rid me, somehow, of the weight
They put upon my small estate
I pruned the first, till it could show
How miniature a heart might grow;
Harnessed the second to a hack
And drove it up the road and back.

Now, with its neatly flowering heart,
My home's a peaceful habitation.
My mind, hitched to its pony cart,
Assures a kind of transportation.
My days are full, my hours are hurried,
Keeping one trimmed, the other curried.
And this is labeled Compensation.

FOREBODING

Life has been such a pleasant host,
So irreproachable, thus far,
I cannot help but wonder what
His ultimate intentions are.

Life has behaved so well, almost
It shames me, to suspect, the while,
There could be any menace shut
Behind his careful smile.

SOME WEALTH MORE SURE

". . . to keep back Beauty, keep it . . ."
GERARD MANLEY HOPKINS

Find something equal to replace
The shape of beauty in your face.
This transient honor time disproves.
Oh, is there not some worthier gift,
Some canceling comfort better still,
More durable to serve, to lift,
To minister to your self, your loves?
This is too slight to wring you so,
(I say) that time has done you ill;
(I say) that beauty is brought low,
That the high breast, the cheek, the thigh
Will droop, fade, slacken; the curved arm
And kindling hands less quick, less warm;
The guarded panic in the eye
Tell you again the thing you know.
Oh find some wealth more sure, more true . . .
Poor woman. Poor myself. Poor you
Who read, if you be woman, too.

THE CRY

Credit me that at least I was prepared
For what time does to beauty in its flesh;
To the round arm, and to the warm round breast;
That though I raged, at least I made the best
Of an unequal conflict, stood and stared
My enemy in the face, and breathed afresh,
Taking some comfort from the strengthening thought
That all's not lost, though beauty come to naught.

But Oh God help me, that I stubbornly dreamed
The heart in the bosom lovely to the last,
The spirit forever ageless and unlined;
Nor ever guessed I might see limping past
On thickened ankles, shabby and winded and lamed,
The light-foot, roebuck-sinewed, leaping mind.

THE LIE

Inland, remembering that coast, I say that I would go
Back to a place I knew,
Stony and dangerous, the bluffs with the sea below
Crashing among the rocks, the long swell churning
Tide-wrack and sand and foam at the wave's dark turning . . .
I say, but it is not true.

Remembering those cliffs, the headlands in the wind,
The hollows of bent grass,
Some breath of that brave violence shakes my mind.
I wish I might climb those slopes again, clinging
To the granite's face, above the sheer drop, my ears ringing—
I wish— But the feeling will pass.

Song, who has left me, was my companion then.
To find her, I would take
Those perilous, stormy, beautiful heights again,
And Death a shifted pebble away. But the nights are colder.
I go indoors, I light the lamp at my shoulder,
I lean to the fire. And I shall not lie awake
Tonight, nor ever, for a word's, for a love's sake.

FOR POT-BOILING

Behold this scarlet shame,
This sin against the Name:
That with deliberate lime
I snared the brave bird, rhyme,
And did this monstrous wrong
To the light-pinioned song.
Know that the outrage wrought
Was well and subtly taught
By the deft mind, whose art
Betrayed the honest heart
With the entangling phrase,
The syllable's smooth ways,
The honeyed verb, the sweet
Trap for the guileless feet.
See how the innocent guest
Fouls his immaculate breast—
And that were shame enough
For one who spread the stuff,
Not from my self disguised,
And bitterly despised.

THE PERVERSE POET

Alas, how sad a thing!
Now that no heavenly anger sits
Troubling the waters of my wits,
I have no song to sing.

This stupefying wealth
Of happiness has struck me dumb.
Those sweetly jangled nerves are numb
Which were my spirit's health.

No sharp, perceptive pain
Turns in my side. I am not glad
To be so well! I would I had
My old disease again!

TILLER OF SOIL

The field lies fallow, but the thrifty soil
Labors the more profound.
Sturdier rhythms of tremendous toil
Quicken the staunch ground.

Were I of wisdom somewhat stouter steeled,
This fact might prove of worth,
And I should trust the ultimate rich yield
Of the slow earth.

But when the fallow Mind denies the year
I cannot rest, nor sleep,
But harrow the black clods, and plant, and fear,
And watch the earth, and weep.

The Mind lies fallow, and the heart at length
Shrieks to the skies of treason.
Trouble this ground no more. Its gathering strength
Waits the new season.

THE POET

I am so lonely, that to bribe my fellows
I tear off bits and splinters of my mind,
Or of my heart, whichever's first at hand,
And build a fire, and pump upon the bellows
To make it bright, that thus I may beguile
These passers-by to lounge about my hearth
(Its fagots I, for what my burning's worth)
And warm their careless fingers, for a while.

47

ASSURANCE

What if the notes be few, indeed?
A simple tune, a single key,
A piping on a slender reed?
Must you, for this, refuse to play?
Some virtue to the song inheres,
So it be true, so it be yours. . . .

THE CHANGE

When I was young, my constant guest
Was Doubt, or lively Wrath, or Rue.
Now all my rage is second best,
The knives are blunted at my breast,
And what I read I think is true.

BEGINNER

Now the page is almost turned
On the lesson I have learned.
On the most that I have known:
My familiar flesh and bone.
Level eyes and lifted chin,
Every part of me that is
Written legibly within
This concise parenthesis
Birth, and Death; the two extremes
Of my mortal paragraph
Dotted with an epitaph.

Wherefore I must now, it seems,
Turn my wits and set my hand
To a newer lexicon,
Striving hard to understand
Primary Oblivion,
In the text assigned to me,
Primer of Eternity.

SEASONS OF THE HEART

"What, are there seasons of the heart, as well?
And how does one, not weather-wise, foretell?
Must I consider, setting out the rose,
A certain frost, inevitable snows?"

PROBLEM

Who can define me Love,
The elements thereof?
What sublety unmesh
This curious riddle, flesh?

If there be one who knows
Let him explain the plan
Whereby the two transpose
Immortal gods, and man!

UNSOPHISTICATE

Ingenuous is the heart,
Naive beyond belief;
Unskilled in the concealment of
Its joy, its grief.

A shrug, a lift of the brow
Are things indeed
Of which the heart
Has need.

TELL ME, GYPSY . . .

And if, my lady, it be Love you're after,
You'll seldom find him in the city square.
Oh many a lordly fellow will be there,
But not the lad; he wearies of light laughter

And jostling to and fro. He likes it quiet,
And rarely feasts with dame and knight and squire,
But sits contented by some cottage fire
And is most happy on a frugal diet.

Love wears no mask, nor any hood to guise him,
And when he knocks, as he has done before,
So neighbor-like upon your bolted door,
Be careful, lady, that you recognize him.

CONCERNING CUPID

Believe me, sir, the little god, I swear
Is guileless as the unsuspicious day.
No malice lurks behind his innocent air,
Nor is he cruel, as some are wont to say
Who find the lily crumpled on its stem,
The shattered heart he toppled from its place,
And forthwith and right speedily condemn
One who is neither treacherous, nor base,

But careless, just like any little boy,
Who, taking up his sling, or bow and arrow,
Goes blithely seeking what he may destroy,
And blinks back tears, above the murdered sparrow.
So, I suspect, doth Venus's small son,
Standing aghast, seeing what he has done!

FOR A MISUNDERSTANDING,
SETTLED UPON THE SPOT

Not I, dear love, who railed upon you thus,
Not you, dealing those bitter words. Instead
A venomous thing that reared its evil head
Between the two of us.

So dark, so deadly, that in truth we knew
One greater than our little grievance nigh.
Thank God we had the courage, you and I,
To thrust it straightly through!

TO ONE WHO OVERLOOKS MY FAULTS

I heard it said that Love had lost his sight,
And could not judge aright.
Nothing could be more false! Love is not blind,
But only very kind.
For, on occasion, I have seen him place
His hands before his face,
And turn away, in utmost charity,
From what he *would* not see.

AFTER QUARRELING

Oh Little Love, it was such foolish railing,
Such bitter things we never meant to say—
And have we frightened you so far away?
Are all our prayers and tears so unavailing?
And have you left no tiniest trace behind you,
That we, who seek you sorrowing, may find you?

REQUIEM

So do we fold the hands of our little Love.
They are quiet now, the narrow, delicate hands.
They will not lift again, nor quiver, nor move
In the old way. Never across the sands
The slender feet of our Love turning home again
Weary, his loose hair blowing back from his brow.
He was wilful, our young-limbed Love, he was hard to restrain,
He roamed too far and too long. It is ended now.
He was always a frail child, he has drooped before,
But we healed him; we knelt at his bed; anguished, we gave
Our two hearts' succor. It was vain at the last. No more.
He lies in so small, so piteously small a grave. . . .

OBJECT LESSON

The snail is cautiously disposed,
His shape is bounded by a shell.
His soft, amorphous self's enclosed
Within a house that serves him well.

You, too, shelled heart, beware the false
Confiding impulse. You will be
Once out of your befriending walls
As naked, lost, betrayed as he.

OUT OF THE BLUE

The hour is come upon me like a hawk
Out of the blue— Oh unsuspecting chick,
Clucking and scratching by the garden walk
No shadow fell across the sun-washed brick
To flatten you against the kindly ground.
Only, in one stunned breath, the air was filled
With a dark, arrowy Presence, and the sound
Of plummet-dropping doom, that clutched and stilled
Your little gasping cry; nor lingered over
The few small feathers on the bloody clover.

WELL LOST FOR LOVE

How many a fervent spirit, in time past,
Challenged the stars; how many a reckless lover
Shattered the sky with such a trumpet blast
As would have toppled Jericho thrice over,
Yet found himself defeated, at the end,
His sword in splinters and his banners furled.
"Counting the world well lost for love . . ." my friend,
The pity is, we may not lose the world.

Turn, if you will, the face of Love away,
Muffle his too-quick ears with desperate laughter,
Dazzle his eyes with passion for a day,
You cannot keep him blind forever after.
Of the relentless shadow on the stair
The happy hour itself will be aware.

NO PHANTOM

This is no phantom at my shoulder blade,
Blotting my piteous shadow with his own;
This is no pale and disembodied shade
Haunting my castle with his troubled moan,
But one whom I most grievously have known,
By whom I have been oftenest dismayed—
A thing in more than transient dust arrayed,
And realer than my personal flesh and bone.

Conscience, or Truth—whichever you prefer.
He never *was* a ghost, with bony hand
Striking such terror in the breast of her
Whose anguished heart could easier withstand
The loudest clank that any sepulcher
Might send at midnight through a startled land.

FIELD OF HONOR

I

In truth, we might have seen it, from the start.
This path would have its turning; there would be
No real alternative for you and me
Fashioned of honest earth, except to part.
Whether the blow were mine to deal, or whether
Yours the swift blade by which this bond were
    sundered,
The hearts must bleed, because the feet have blundered
Into a way we may not walk together.

Rebuke me not, beloved, in that I
Perforce do quickly that which needs must be;
I am as one who fights because she fears
A darker wound, a deadlier agony
Than fronts her now—and if I say good-by,
Believe me that I say it through my tears.

II

I do beseech that you believe me true,
And cry your solace in my desperate need.
My dearest love, I had been false indeed
If I did not this bitter thing I do.
Better a thousand times the anguish due,
The heart insolvent, but the spirit freed,
Than turn thus traitor to a certain creed,
And faithless to myself, as well as you.

64

For it were surely treachery most base
To risk the sullying of so proud a shield;
To chance a single stain upon the face
Of what we bear in honor from the field,
Worthy to keep untarnished through the years,
Though polished daily with what meed of tears.

III

Strange paradox, my friend, that you and I
Who deemed our trusted strength so sure and sweet,
Must find ourselves stricken to earth thereby,
Our swords turned sharply to our own defeat.
"Wisdom" writ large across the frozen breast
Is doubtful comfort when the heart is breaking;
What final irony is manifest
That we are scourged with thongs of our own making.

So I shall nevermore behold your face,
Nor look for heaven at your fingertips;
And all my ordered goings shall attest
How I have set mine honor in its place!
Albeit by the blood upon my lips,
Albeit by the ashes in my breast.

ON THE PERSPECTIVE OF GRIEF

The shape and hue of pain
Demand a stricter eye
Than the too biased brain
Can properly supply,

So close confronting grief
It fails to see the art
Of what stands hugely in relief
Against the tortured heart.

THE SILENT ONES

The rapt breast falters at the notes
That soar too full and free;
They do not sing of love, whose throats
Are thick with ecstasy.
And when the temple riven stands,
And when the God departs,
They do not speak of grief, whose hands
Are clenched against their hearts.

A LONG TIME AFTER

Being a woman, with a woman's art
She kept the unforgotten word from rust,
Albeit justified by no sane reason
For folding it thus tenderly apart;
Knowing so sadly well, as women must,
Love's little guile, his unintended treason.
But with no rancor at her wistful heart
Taking in gentle hands the fragrant dust
Of what *was* surely Truth, once, for a season. . . .

ADVICE TO A LADY

For that you are so bruised and sore,
And do so long to ease your ache,
Lady, be careful all the more
What remedies you take.

For that you hunger, Lady, heed
To that degree, and do not haste
To nibble any crust, lest need
Itself have dulled your taste.

By nature wanting to believe,
To tend an altar, and to pray,
Watch—lest your faithful hands contrive
Another god of clay.

ADVICE TO A GENTLEMAN

The lady's heart is shy and wary of capture,
Entreat her subtly, stalk her like a fawn.
She will be most beguiled by crumbs of rapture,
By the potentials, by the feast withdrawn.

She is beset with curious alarm,
She cannot tell what is her hunger and drouth.
Assure her of the circle of your arm,
And touch her breast but do not kiss her mouth.

It is hard for her to say to any man.
Her quivering need of flight is not of reason.
There are no words shadowy enough to explain—
And she will give you her lips in due season.

Attend her, she will come to you in her fashion.
She is restive and mobile, but she is not dissembling.
Love her, if she be worth your trouble and passion,
But do not hold her against her body's trembling.

THE PROPITIATOR

Once, long ago, in bitter grief I said
"This is the ultimate pain.
Nothing henceforth that life can do to me
Will hurt so much, again . . ."

I wish today I knew some rune, some charm,
Could some oblation make,
Lest listening God or demon tempted be
To show me my mistake!

THANKSGIVING

Oh I have railed before at God,
And I shall rail at Him again,
Because so heavy lies His rod
Upon my myriad fellow men—

But I have warmth and food and drink,
I have my love, who loveth me—
The which is chief and best, I think,
Of any blessing that could be.

And in such wealth forgetting all,
That good men have so little good,
Down on my selfish knees I fall
And am engulfed in gratitude.

3 A.M.

Night has an entity, a shape
Of darkness, skeletoned with fear,
And few there be who can escape
Some chill acquaintanceship with her.

Night has a manner of speech, a voice
Which she can properly disguise:
A mouse's bickering, the small noise
Of crumbling embers, or the sighs

In empty corners, or the squeaks
Of doors ajar at no one's hand.
In such masked syllables night speaks,
And all her listeners understand.

Yet, when I lie with you, my love,
Curved to your side, and warm, and well,
So proud, so gracious night doth move
I'd swear she were an archangel,

Who otherwhile were grim to hear,
A bodiless presence in the gloom,
And heavy on the frightened ear
Her subtle footfall through the room.

BRIGHT FACE OF DANGER

No woman born was ever glad
To have this sense of peril nigh,
Like lightning, insolent and bad,
Flaring its signals in her sky.

Yet I, like women everywhere,
Find something in this danger good.
The spiced, the thunder-freighted air
Sends an elixir through the blood.

So fine a fury never was
The gift of safe and shining day
Whose light lay on the quiet grass
Dreaming its numbered hours away.

Oh thank the prick, the feel of harm,
This violent and bitter weather,
That we lock fingers, arm in arm,
And walk into the wind, together.

PREMONITION

This is the first faint omen of the storm:
An indefinable altering of the air,
The feeling rather than the visible form
Of danger; and the watcher is aware
Of a mute, troubled prescience everywhere,
As if the grasses and the wise trees knew,
But could not warn him when he turns to stare
In apprehension at the faithless blue.

So does the heart presage its gathering grief,
In signs as subtly ominous as a leaf
Loosed from a tremulous bough, and fluttering lightly
Down to the earth. Now, in this waiting weather,
The heart, disquieted, waits too—and rightly
Peers at the sky, and strikes its hands together.

THE WIND

All night the dark wind blows,
Roars through the bending boughs,
And like a great sea throws
Its weight against the house.

Time was, I could have heard
That fury of the air
And slept again, unstirred;
Who now awake, aware

Of other storms than are
Out of air's warring made,
And deadlier by far,
Lie sleepless and afraid,

Hearing in this night's wind
A wind that will not rest,
Shaking the frightened mind,
Freezing the breast.

THE WINTER REASON

Now is my garden, summer long
So confident in bloom and leaf,
So unsuspicious of the wrong
Winter would do it, brought to grief.

How, in this brutal season's hold
Can any April hope be sure?
Oh seeds, keep warm beneath the cold,
Oh roots, be strong—endure, endure—

EXPLANATION

Because I have not clutched my throat and cried,
Because I have not shrieked to east and west,
Are you persuaded that the blow went wide,
Or only grazed the breast?

At any moment, now, the ice will go
From the stunned bosom where the blade sank in,
The numbed blood quicken in the veins, and flow,
And the wound throb, and the agony begin.

NATURAL HISTORY NOTE

I like hard things, like bones,
And rocks, and flinty stones. . . .
That I am soft is why, I think, I want
The feel of adamant.

I praise all armored things
With shells, and stings.
That I unguarded was
Must be the cause.

THE HOAX

Paraded grief offends.
So long as I am able,
I shall make my friends
And my guests comfortable.

I can shriek loud and rough
As any beast in pain;
God keep me proud enough
To avoid such a scene.

Grief's ragged wilderness dress,
At best not pretty,
Becomes me even less
Worn formally in the city.

I know what I must do
For my soul's and body's good:
I shall hold my head high,
I shall eat my food.

And yet I recognize
The pitiful paradox
Of hoping someone's eyes
Perceive the hoax;

Wishing, against my will,
That somehow be descried
What, wild and bleeding still,
I strive so hard to hide.

THE DEATH

So firm and strong my love, so surely tested
No power had shaken it, of God or human.
Angels and Principalities it had met, and bested.
Not you, in love's own house turned foeman.

With you on crusts and dregs it would have thrived,
And laughed, and taken its stand.
No wound so vicious it had not survived
Save this—dealt by your hand.

THE WOUND

"And one shall say unto him, What are these wounds
in thine hands? Then he shall answer, Those with
which I was wounded in the house of my friends."

ZECHARIAH 13: 6

I will wash this wound, and bind it with honey and oil.
I will say "It is nothing. Let be. The bleeding will stop."
Knowing I lie in my teeth, that it will not heal
Nor soon, nor ever. It has been torn too deep.
The dark stains widen. . . . I think there is no balm
That the cool mind can bring, no skill, no art
To close this ragged horror in my palm,
To quench the bright blood pounding from the heart.

THE SURVIVOR

When I went through the wilderness
Sustenance, of a sort, I found,
Meager and scanty though it was
Upon that graceless ground.

It did not hang like fruit on trees,
There were no trees in that scarred land;
I sought it on my hands and knees
Among the rocks and sand.

It was no proper kind of food,
That simple Wanting Not To Die,
But every little scrap was good,
So ravenous was I.

And if my pillow was a shard,
From stripped sheer weariness I slept,
And grown so muscular and hard,
How light, how fierce I stepped!

Another Exodus like that
I could not make, and live. And yet
In a green land, and warm, and fat,
I think and think on it. . . .

THE DIFFERENCE

Charity is silent, Charity is content
To have said in silence everything Love meant.
Charity does not seek
A phrase, but sets warm lips upon the cheek.
Even if it rejoice
Love needs no speech, but Rancor wants a voice,
And tirelessly will rehearse
Its grievance, chapter and verse.
Love's mute, and willingly so; but do not doubt
Anger's articulate, and will speak out.
Charity holds its peace, but be assured
Bitterness knows a final, ruinous word,
And Bitterness will, at any cost, be heard.

MEN AND WOMEN

"I thought that nature was enough
Till human nature came . . ."

EMILY DICKINSON

PORTRAIT OF A CERTAIN GENTLEMAN

This man's uncertain; he's afraid
To make a choice which, being made,
He must abide by, bad or good.
So he'd avoid it, if he could.

He'd like to hide away, to run
Out of reality's broad sun
Into a cave, a hole, a crack
In earth's kind substance; he'd go back

To what he fancies was secure,
The state of childhood, which was sure,
Since he was told what he should do.
That world's grown up, the man has, too.

Poor child, poor man, there's no escape
From what is termed your adult shape,
This form which you attain at last
Through such betrayals in the past.

Nor God nor man will tell you, now,
What you must do, or when, or how.
There's no retreat that may be won to,
No one except your self to run to.

PORTRAIT OF A SELFISH MAN

This gentleman was never known to be
False for an instant to the faith that bore him
Ruthless, unswerving, toward a planned objective.
Here was a suave and courteous cruelty,
An ego that illumed the path before him
And showed him man's estate in new perspective.
He would have haled no Christ to Calvary,
Knowing so well that simply to ignore Him
Would be less vulgar—and wholly as effective.

FOR A CERTAIN KINDLY ATHEIST

His heart's Jerusalem of doubt
I cannot ask that Thou condone;
But, if he cast Thy prophets out,
He flung no stone—

He led them to the city gates,
And bade them bind their sandals on,
And gave them bread and wine and dates
Before he said "Begone!"

OF CERTAIN RIGHTEOUS

They walk uprightly, from their youth,
Observing, without fleck or flaw,
Honesty, Virtue, Courage, Truth,
All weightier matters of the Law.

An admirable tribe, and yet
Through accident, or by design,
These worthy folk so oft forget
The pleasant tithes of spice and wine.

CHURCH FUNERAL FOR A
CERTAIN GENTLEMAN

Therein so little of his time was spent,
No doubt his ghost must think it rather odd
That anyone should deem it exigent
To speed his passing from the House of God.
For most commandments of the Holy Writ
He held complete unblushing disregard,
And finding the Seventh particularly hard,
Made his own softer bed, and lay in it.

Praised by the Eulogy, blessed in the Prayer,
Surely his ghost, if it were here today,
The startled honor guest of this affair
Might well have writhed, and wished itself away,
But, courteous as in life, had listened to it,
A trifle bored, perhaps, but smiling through it.

OBJECT LESSON FOR A
CERTAIN GENTLEMAN

From his position on a lilac spray
He stared with cold severity around.
Completed a most critical survey
And seemed dissatisfied with all he found.

What his opinion was, concerning it,
None in the quiet garden cared a fig.
All of which shook his self-esteem no whit,
That pompous insect, strutting on a twig.

PORTRAIT FROM NATURE

I knew a man once, very like that cliff,
And thought of him, seeing the stubborn wall
Bracing the leaning mountain's stony fall,
Solid and stern and confident as if

It propped the sky above the windy crown—
And thought of him again, because I saw
Across the granite's face the ruinous flaw
Which, given its time, would bring the mountain down.

THE MAN WHO TOOK LITERALLY
THE ADVICE
OF THREE MONKEYS

He saw no evil, even when
'T was done before his eyes, for then
With a discreet and courteous grace
He'd tactfully avert his face.

He heard no evil, taking care
To clap a hand upon each ear,
And thus successfully he drowned
Outrageous wrong's unlovely sound.

He praised some good in every man,
Lest he offend him, or his clan,
And sometimes, just by keeping still,
He was absolved of speaking ill.

Oh he was everybody's friend,
And so was no one's, in the end;
And could have better served his kind
Honestly deaf and dumb and blind!

DESTINY

Stricken, from his unequal lot,
Unto the Lord this poor man cried.
God, being busy, heard him not.
Disheartened, the man died.

Years thence, essaying life again,
He drew a jonquil's little breath—
And by the blades of wind and rain
Straightway was done to death.

THE MAN WHO LOVED CARE

Here was a man of whom it might be said
He loved the old drab, Care. Nay, what was more,
He took her lean shanks to his poor bleak bed
And sought to make a good wife of the whore.
Gave her ten tenths of all he had in store,
Poured out the wine of life, and spurned the bread,
Gnawed the sour fruit of pain, and ate the core,
And then, one day, we heard that he was dead.

And so we dug a grave and laid him in
With less of moan than is at times the case,
And there was none to lend him that last grace
Of tears; for she who was his love, and sin,
Left him to brawl with death for his bones' worth,
And whine and scratch at the cold roof of earth.

PORTRAIT OF A CERTAIN LADY

"She was so gentle, and so piteous
She would weep, if that she saw a mouse
Caught in a trap, if it were dead, or bled . . ."

CHAUCER

For mice, caged brutes, for trampled worms,
She could an instant pity find.
But never saw in equal terms
Their parallels in human kind.

She had a cool, a pure disdain.
This lady never understood
The inner hurt, the secret pain
Which makes men savage, stupid, rude.

A beast in agony may snap
At the extended rescuing hand,
But human creatures, in a trap,
Should have more courage at command.

Because the fallacy's abroad
That man, the rational creature, springs
Whole-natured from the hand of God,
Why, cornered men are different things!

Yet mangled spirits may behave
With less calm judgment than is right.
Anguish is seldom wise or brave,
Agony is not even polite.

Madame, this man who snarls in pain,
Who tramps rough-footed through your house,
Although his wound show not so plain,
Can bleed as well as any mouse!

PORTRAIT OF A LADY

Madame has put to shame the prophet's verse.
She is, I think, a very silken purse.
Though the materials involved, and how,
The lady's not inclined to mention now.
She keeps a regal manner in employ,
A delicate disdain for *hoi polloi*,
Poor honest swine she finds it such a bore
To cast, at times, her cultured pearls before.

FOR A SPINSTER, DYING OF CANCER
OF THE BREAST

Alack, what irony. is this!
Surely a harsh and bitter jest
That one inviolate so long
Should come at last to such a lover.
Here was a very virgin breast,
A heart no passion might discover,
Whom death has done a cruel wrong,
Betrayed unto a brutal kiss.
Dishonored, now, and given over,
Finally, shamefully possessed.

PROBLEM FOR THE PSYCHIATRIST

She kept the shining cupboards of her mind
Spotless, with an unceasing diligence,
And, spinster-souled, dwelt tidily behind
The delicate closed doors of reticence.
Her orderly emotions she arrayed
In rows, each in its little labeled jar
Like jelly, and her calm desires she laid
Carefully pressed, away in lavender.

But in a corner of a secret shelf
She kept a vial, wrought in curious fashion,
The deadly brew of a most bitter passion.
And no one ever knew, besides herself,
What agony of care she had to take
Lest, some unguarded hour, it leak, or break.

TO AN OLD WOMAN ON THE SUBWAY

You should have shiny pewter,
And a table spread,
The smell of new baking,
And a tall bed—

Kettle and friendly tea
Chatting together—
You should never be
Out in such weather!

You, with chill hands clasped
And an anxious eye
Trying to see what station
Has just flashed by.

PUBLIC FIGURE

"The hermit crab, having no shell of its own,
appropriates the empty shells of other creatures,
in which it takes up residence. . . ."

NATURAL HISTORY NOTE

Since I myself no armor had
To bind about my skin,
I found a neighbor's outgrown shell
And promptly moved therein.

And so adjustable was I
(Lacking a rigid bone)
I fitted every coil and groove
As it had been my own.

Now, though my fine and lustrous walls
Contain no stuff of me,
How passionately I affirm
Our single entity!

THE PRUDENT MAN

Preferring not to risk a nasty fall
In the event he missed his step, or slipped,
He looked so thoroughly before he leapt
That, in the end, he did not leap at all.
His chickens could be counted on; he kept
Their eggs in cartons stacked against the wall,
And, lest his horse be stolen, he equipped
The barn with triple locks, and wired the stall.

He made his bed, and in it soundly slept
Until one night an unaccustomed chill
Nagged at his bones, and in his bosom crept.
But, since the difference was so slight and small,
He never knew his ticking heart had stopped,
And that his close-drawn blanket was his pall.

OGRE'S CASTLE

Guests in that household learned to hang their clothes
On hooks in the wall, or over the back of a chair,
Not in the closets, from which unpleasantly rose
A charnel smell, like something moldering there.
The host's strange predilection for suspending
Swords from the rafters overhead unnerved them,
But they got used to it, and to pretending
They liked boiled crow, the dish most frequently served them.

They found it tactful, when the farmer's sheep
Went bleating by, to ignore among the flock
A certain lupine slant of eye and jaw;
And even the dullest grasped the unwritten law:
Not twice in a single night to wake the cock,
Or rouse the mastiffs, whimpering in their sleep.

OBSERVATION

"Scientists warn against looking directly at the
eclipse, even through smoked glasses. Serious damage
to the retina will result."

NEWS NOTE

Not Gods, nor mortal man,
When in eclipse, care to be so defined,
And in retaliation, if they can,
Will strike the gazer blind.

COUNSEL

Women, especially wives, should never fight
For what they consider, however justly, a right,
But pursue the point with delicacy and tact,
And never confound a gentleman with a fact.

Women must learn, albeit with some pain,
That a principle for a principle's sake is vain.
They will not lose their soul's integrity
By giving ground, and giving graciously.

Women and men, not excepting husbands and wives,
Have a deep core of separateness in their lives.
It is a place where neither one should tread,
No matter how many years they have shared one bed.

And it is woman's part, I think, to observe
Such boundaries, and to know when to swerve,
When to stop short, go around, keep silent, take
A little defeat for her own, for her love's sake.

ED JONES 1933
BILL SMITH 1936
JIM TURNER 1928

A curious panic in the mind
Afflicts the humblest human creature.
Sensing the transience of his nature,
Man cannot rest until he find

Some means to stake his ego's claim,
His point in time—although it be
But scratching on some sturdy tree
His brief, his unenduring name.

THE MAN NAMED LEGION

The man named Legion asks for nothing more
Than his own rooftree, and the right to stand
Erect, unthreatened, on a square of land,
His children sturdy, and his peace secure.
The world is wide, the generous earth could nourish
All men, and more, and still have room to spare.
So brief a time is his to breathe the air,
So cheap, so simple, all that he would cherish.

Out of such modest stuff his dreams are made,
But being humble, he is set at naught,
Harried, despoiled, most grievously betrayed,
And the pathetic little that he sought
Is set beyond his hope, beyond his touch.
That little—that impossible too much!

ON CONTEMPLATING AN OPEN FIRE

Man, the supreme sophisticate,
Inhabiting his world, transfuses
Its elements to his own uses,
Disguising their original state.
He builds his house of brick and steel,
Heaps concrete on the simple grass,
Traps lightning in a globe of glass,
On the four winds he sets his heel.
The rivers in their beds he chastens,
The foaming cataract restrains,
It turns his factories' wheels, or drains
Demurely into porcelain basins.
He halts the seasons in their spinnings,
Indoors, at least, no winters find him.
Nothing he does serves to remind him
Of his primordial beginnings,
Except that, with the will to tame
And alter everything he touches,
He still piles log on log, and crouches
Before the elemental flame.

SALUTE TO MAN

I think that surely God in heaven
Must marvel out His creatures' courage!
Let but a shred of light be given,
How they pursue it! How they forage
Among the meager sheaves of Chance
To glean a stalk; how they stand up
And hurl the glove at Circumstance.
And if on crusts and dregs they sup
They talk of faith, and turn their eyes
To that far hinterland of hope
Towards which, indomitably, they grope.
They stumble, fall; but watch them rise
And brush the blood and dust away.
"It could be worse," they stoutly say.
Oh God, how proud You ought to be
Of these who clutch Thy garment's hem,
Who struggle grimly after Thee.
The morning stars must sing for them!

EX TENEBRIS

I

Ex Tenebris

I was a long time dying, and the gold
I saved for such a misadventure proved
Less durable than I. Now, from my mold,
I send this counsel to my upright kin,
(So they may wiser be than I have been):
See to it that yourselves grow never old
Nor luckless, nor unlovely and unloved.

II

What the Medium Said

Because I'd always been a sturdy fellow
I hardly understood
That sudden waking to a sodden pillow
And the brass taste of blood.

You see, I wasn't one for babying,
Nor easy terrified—
So I was more surprised than anything,
The night I died.

HIC JACET

I

Epitaph for a Certain Gentleman

Here lieth one whose fleshly lust
Did always his meek spirit lead.
Now, meditating in the dust,
He finds it comforting to trust

A Christ who was not too divine
To recognize a human need,
But went with Publicans to dine,
And turned the water into wine.

II

Epitaph for a Certain Lady

What if she were not too wise?
This is all that need be said:
She was lovely. . . . and she lies
Strangely in a narrow bed
Where the lusty worms attest
To the softness of her breast.

III

Epitaph for a Little Grave

The busy crickets, all day long,
Chirrup an unmolested song
Here where the grasses wave
O'er one who only lived until
He grew quite tall enough to fill
A little two-foot grave.

111

GRASSHOPPER IN THE CEMETERY

I rather think he saw the joke,
With other less explicit folk—
This gentleman in gray and brown
Who from his grass-stalk clambered down,
Read what the marble had to say,
Spat on the ground, and turned away.

EPITAPH FOR A SPINSTER

I was virgin all my life,
No man wanted me to wife.

Never man's head came to rest
On the shadow of my breast.

Therefore, I shall make a most
Tractable, contented ghost

With no certain pangs to start
Knocking at my dusty heart.

In the dark, I shall not cry.
Tell me, Gabriel, how could I

Who have lain so long alone
Miss what I have never known?

Master, on that Final Day
When you tilt the clouds away

I shall scramble from my mold,
Self-sufficient, as of old,

One who, though shut out, at least
Missed the turmoil of the feast.

Something You could scarcely call
Wholly foolish, after all!

BOY IN THE WOODS

The lad was straight and sturdy grown,
With a lean-muscled grace of limb,
He took the wooded path alone,
And his stout fancy strode with him.

She buckled rawhide at his wrist
And wrapped fringed leggings on his shins,
She thrust a rifle in his fist
And shod his feet with moccasins.

He moved like shadow, or a snake,
And lightly as a dappled fawn
He crossed the hollow and the brake
And leapt the covert, and was gone. . . .

Till at his own back gate he stood
Alert and poised as though there still
Were Indians in the darkening wood
And catamounts upon the hill.

TO MY SMALL SON, BUSY IN
THE BACK YARD

Here is the spot where fifty dragons died,
Yesterday morning, shortly after ten,
And here the trampled grass, on every side,
Was reddened with the blood of gentlemen
Nobler than ever rode beneath the sky,
Braver than Arthur's knights could ever be.
(Or so I am informed. And who am I
To doubt the tale as it was told to me?)

Nay, I am quite convinced. The thing is true.
Never such deeds were done as you rehearse.
But come, proclaim a truce this hour or two,
Scowl not upon a cringing universe,
Lord of the Back Yard and the Nursery,
Guzzler of Jello, Toper of Cambric Tea.

TO MY SMALL SON, IN CHURCH

In the brief space of half an hour, not more,
You have constructed paper hats, and ships,
Managed to drop my purse upon the floor,
Reduced the Bulletin to ragged strips,
And from what next will fire your nimble mind,
I shrink with a maternal apprehension.
Assuredly, in church, my son, I find
Monotony the mother of invention.

Now, shorn of hymnal and collection folder,
The final hope of occupation gone,
With conversation being frowned upon
Your interest, if possible, grows colder.
You glance despairingly at me, and yawn,
Slide glumly down, and sleep against my shoulder.

TO MY SMALL SON, BEACH-COMBING

The sea has treasures, ingots of bright gold,
Coffers of silver coins and jeweled rings,
Rubies, and carven jade, and precious things
More than your pockets, more than a house could hold.
She hides them in her glimmering icy caves,
They lie long fathoms down, the dark weeds bind them,
And you and I, my son, will never find them
Flung on the beaches by the careless waves.

But she will give us a stone rubbed smooth and shining,
Keeping its colors even when it is dry,
And a periwinkle's roof, like a little bell,
And an oyster's empty hinge with its pearly lining,
And a wisp of sponge, and a marvelous fluted shell
With the sound of her voice therein, to remember her by.

TO MY SMALL SON, ROLLER-SKATING

Doubtless the fault is mine, not having mentioned
Upon the list of things I prayed the fates
Would not present, this pair of roller-skates,
Donation not so wise as well-intentioned.
The strange part is that I as yet am sane
While watching you careening down the street,
And wondering just how long you will remain
Upon your most unmanageable feet.

But latent masculinity has girt you
In mail of such impregnable design
That you can tumble flat, oh son of mine,
And quite refuse to let it disconcert you.
Or, having all but fractured your small spine,
Can blink back tears, and swear it did not hurt you!

TO MY SMALL SON, ON
CERTAIN OCCASIONS

When you, my son, were very, very young,
I was intrigued and mystified, to see
With what an odd persistency you clung
To a remembrance of identity.
As if some other You lay snugly curled
Behind your strangely contemplative eyes,
And stared incuriously upon the world,
Aloof, remote, inordinately wise.

Now, though a certain naughtiness enjoys
The greater part of everything you do;
Though washed, fed, spanked and taught like all small boys,
Sometimes the old, old look returns to you.
And, coming unawares upon it, I
Am suddenly abashed, not knowing why.

TO MY SMALL SON, GROWING UP

". . . but when I became a man, I put away childish things."

I CORINTHIANS 13: 11

God grant he may not lose them, yet,
All of the little childish things.
I cannot bear that he forget
His young and brave imaginings.

That, growing up, he lose them quite:
The splendid, marching days that pass,
The Pirate in the wind at night,
The curious, friendly fingered grass.

Is it such wisdom, that he can
At so great price, become a man?

ANOTHER STORY

"But that, O Best Beloved, is another story."

RUDYARD KIPLING. JUST SO STORIES

DEDICATION

To all the luckless suitors who died trying
To scale a slope of glass;
To poor Rapunzel, in her tower sighing,
To Abelard, at Mass;
To Dido, on the headlands, hearing the dying
Sound of the oarlocks' ring,
And little Abishag, into her pillows crying,
Warming an old, cold King. . . .*

* I Kings 1: 1, 2, 3

THE BUILDERS

I told them a thousand times if I told them once:
Stop fooling around, I said, with straw and sticks;
They won't hold up. You're taking an awful chance.
Brick is the stuff to build with, solid bricks.
You want to be impractical, go ahead,
But just remember, I told them; wait and see.
You're making a big mistake. Awright, I said,
But when the wolf comes, don't come running to me.

The funny thing is, they didn't. There they sat,
One in his crummy yellow shack, and one
Under his roof of twigs, and the wolf ate
Them, hair and hide. Well, what is done is done.
But I'd been willing to help them, all along,
If only they'd once admitted they were wrong.

SYNDICATED COLUMN

Dear Worried: Your husband's actions aren't unique,
His jealousy's a typical defense.
He feels inadequate; in consequence,
He broods. (My column, by the way, last week
Covered the subject fully.) I suggest
You reassure him; work a little harder
To build his ego, stimulate his ardor,
Lose a few pounds, and try to look your best.

As for his growing a beard, and dyeing it blue,
Merely a bid for attention; nothing wrong with him.
Stop pestering him about that closet, too,
If he wants to keep it locked, why, go along with him.
Just be the girl he married; don't nag, don't pout.
Cheer up. And let me know how things work out.

DR. S— INTERVIEWS A
WORRIED MOTHER

Madame, your little girl's extreme aversion
To a quite bland, innocuous nursery dish,
Stems, we suggest, from her subconscious wish
To punish you for some alleged incursion
Upon her ego. Real or fancied hurt
Often assumes this curious disguise.
Three sibling cats we know won't touch dessert,
Due to an early trauma involving pies.

The child's insistence that a horrid creature
Scared her at lunch is plainly the transfer
Of a repressed hostility which seeks
Symbology of an acceptable nature.
Bring her in every day for the next few weeks;
I'd like to find out what's *really* troubling her.

LOCAL BOY MAKES GOOD

I hear he's changed a lot since he's been grown.
You'd never know him now, but *I* recall
He used to be so timid and so small
He'd hardly dare to call his soul his own.
I guess we bullied him, but who'd have thought
That he'd be rich and famous, one fine day?
And handsome, into the bargain, so they say.
I don't begrudge him anything he's got,

But all the same, I'd rather like to remind him
That though we're proud of him, and wish him luck,
Here in the poultry yard he left behind him
He'll always be that scrawny little duck
All bones and pinfeathers and yellow fuzz,
Who couldn't tell you who his father was.

THE SLEEPER

I

(She speaks)

I wish the Prince had left me where he found me,
Wrapped in a rosy trance so charmed and deep
I might have lain a hundred years asleep.
I hate this new and noisy world around me.
The palace hums with sightseers from town,
There's not a quiet spot that I can find.
And, worst of all, he's chopped the brambles down . . .
The lovely briars I've felt so safe behind.

But if he thinks that with a kiss or two
He'll buy my dearest privacy, or shake me
Out of the cloistered world I've loved so long,
Or break the pattern of my dream, he's wrong.
Nothing this clumsy trespasser can do
Will ever touch my heart, or really wake me.

II

(He speaks)

I used to think that slumberous look she wore,
The dreaming air, the drowsy-lidded eyes,
Were artless affectation, nothing more.
But now, and far too late, I realize
How sound she sleeps, behind a thorny wall
Of rooted selfishness, whose stubborn strands
I broke through once, to kiss her lips and hands
And wake her heart, that never woke at all.

I wish I'd gone away that self-same hour,
Before I learned how, like her twining roses,
She bends to her own soft, implacable uses
The pretty tactics that such vines employ,
To hide the poisoned barb beneath the flower,
To cling about, to strangle, to destroy.

THE INVESTIGATOR

It's unprovoked and wanton cruelty.
In the first place, the unfortunate mice were blind;
They couldn't have chased her, since they couldn't see
Which way to jump. And secondly, what kind
Of woman is she, to take a carving knife
And maim them so? I never saw a more
Pitiful spectacle in all my life
Than those three tails, limp on the bloody floor.

Maybe she likes to hear things run and squeak . . .
But if it's really *mice* she hates like that,
She could set traps, or keep a hungry cat.
There's more to this, perhaps, than meets the eye.
Her husband's not been seen since Monday week.
I think I'll stop by the farm and find out why.

I REMEMBER MAMA

The trouble is, I never felt secure.
There we were, crammed into that wretched shoe,
Ragged and cold and miserably poor,
And Mama never knowing what to do.
Most of the time we lived on watery stew,
She couldn't even bake a loaf of bread,
And every night she'd thrash us black and blue
And send the sniveling lot of us to bed.

I used to lie awake for hours, and plan
The things I'd do, when I became a man . . .
And this is why I lurk in darkened hallways
And prowl dim streets and lonely parks, and always
Carry a knife, in case I meet another
Old woman who reminds me of my mother.

THE PRINCESS

I'll ask for a red rose blossoming in the snow,
A music box hid in a walnut shell,
Nine golden apples on a silver bough,
A mirror that can speak, and cast a spell.
I'll send them East of the Moon, and West of the Sun
For a wishing ring made of a dragon's claw. . . .
And they will fail, just as the rest have done,
And I can stay at home, with dear Papa.

Oh sometimes in my silken bed I wake
All of a shiver, and my hair on end,
Because again the terrible dream occurred:
What if one of those suitors *should* come back
With the impossible trophy in his hand,
And I should have to keep my foolish word!

ONLY SON

I want you all to meet Thomas, my son.
One moment, till I lift my thumb a bit,
Now you can see him better, under it . . .
That's where I keep him. Don't you think I've done
A marvelous job in pruning him so small
Without his feeling any pain at all?
It took, of course, maternal dedication,
A velvet claw, and tireless concentration.

And here he stands, my tiny pride and joy.
We're more like sweethearts than like son and mother.
He'd rather be with me than any other.
He's thirty-seven, but he's still my boy.
He'd sooner die, he says, than hurt or grieve me—
Isn't he darling? And he'll never leave me.

WELFARE REPORT

Folks down the road thought something must be wrong
After the dog kept coming, night after night,
Nosing about for scraps; and they were right.
I don't know how she'd managed for so long.
The stove was cold, the kindling all used up,
The cupboard bare, not even so much as a bone,
And nobody else in the house; just her alone
And that old collie she's had since he was a pup.

She'll be much better off at the County Home,
And she'll have to accept the fact that they couldn't keep
A perfectly worthless hungry old dog around.
We had him put to sleep at the local pound
Before he bit somebody or started to roam,
Chasing the neighbors' chickens, or running sheep.

THE WITCH

It pleases me to give a man three wishes,
Then trick him into wasting every one.
To set the simpering goosegirl on the throne
While the true princess weeps among the ashes.
I like to come unbidden to the christening,
Cackling a curse on the young princeling's head,
To slip a toad into the maiden's bed,
To conjure up the briers, the glass slope glistening.

And I am near, oh nearer than you've known.
You cannot shut me in a fairy book.
It was my step you heard, mine and my creatures',
Soft at your heel. And if you lean and look
Long in your mirror, you will see my features
Inextricably mingled with your own.

BIRDS AND BEASTS

"The birds and the beasts were there . . ."

THE CURLEW

A curlew, scouting for his flock,
Came on me suddenly, as I
Sat staring at the sea and sky,
And perched upon a rock

Not twenty paces from my hand.
And, since I did not stir or speak,
He smoothed his feathers with his beak,
And skipped along the sand,

And with a bright, unstartled eye
Observed this stranger on his beach,
Then made a little chattering speech
And teetered delicately

Upon his reedy legs. Unknown
Although my status was, his guess
Was that I had some business
With sea, or were a stone

Unswayed by any winds that blow
From what dark wastes of north or east,
Solid and sure and safe—at least
He judged me to be so.

PIGEON ENGLISH

The plump, the pompous-bosomed bird
Perches upon the steepled roof.
He wears a look of mild reproof
And speaks in accents soft and blurred.
One melancholy theme is his:
"And the difficulty is . . . and the difficulty is . . ."

His neighbor sits and cocks an eye
Upon the crowded street below.
He sees the people come and go,
He feels Time's feathered wing brush by.
Nods his head sagely, and says he:
"Indubitably . . . indubitably . . ."

FOR A LITTLE BIRD THAT BLUNDERED INTO CHURCH

God, that harnesseth the winds,
And the lordly striding sun,
Turn from heaven a little space,
Pity this, Thy frightened one.

Thou Who knowest the sparrow's way,
Set these beating pinions free—
God, if Thou art in Thy house,
Show him where the windows be!

THE PESSIMIST

An agèd fly sat on my wrist today,
Survived, somehow, till April had begun.
But he was very old and stiff and gray,
And Time had warped his knee joints, every one.
So still he sat, I almost feared him dead,
But feebly chafing his front legs together,
He rubbed them querulously o'er his head.
"Heigh-ho—" he sighed, "it's nice here in the sun."
I cocked an ear to catch what he might say.
"God knows it's hard to spend six months abed
Only to greet old age in April weather.
We flies are heaven's private jest," he said,
"Her laughing stock, Fate's whimsy gone astray."
He rose, with ancient bitterness bestead,
Heaved up his wings and weakly buzzed away.

FOR A LOCUST THAT DIED, EMERGING FROM ITS CHRYSALIS

Behold the dark duplicity of nature.
Here lieth one whose little life was spent
In a pathetic singleness of striving
Towards a Supreme Event.

The animate womb which was his own small body
Conceived himself mysteriously in earth,
To perish thus, in strange and bitter travail,
Bringing himself to birth!

FOR A PRAYING MANTIS, ON A CITY STREET

Alas, my friend, what ill wind brought you here,
Into an alien region, for no good?
Lost and bewildered, for what mighty Ear
Do you assume the ancient attitude?

There is small comfort for the bitter mind
Which reads your lesson on a larger scale,
And thinks what countless other hands have joined
In the same gesture, and to like avail.

THE SNAIL

And here the ultimate example is
Of Ego—an existence centered wholly
Within itself. Behold this gentleman,
The perfect introvert. Why, he is his
Own hearth and rooftree, not to say the span
Of all his universe. The melancholy
Tumult of obligation does not stir
The esoteric calm of one who can
Affirm identity so sure and fast
As to become, at last,
Himself his sepulcher.

LITTLE FABLE

"Friend," said the panther to the snail,
"I pity you the life you lead,
So cramped, so thwarted by a shell.
You should be freed.

"How sad that you thus meekly go,
Undaring, circumscribed and slow.
I dare, *I* leap, I make my kill,
I do my will."

"True," said the snail, "a just reproof."
He strained against his little roof,
Uncoiled himself, and with a shout
Stepped out.

He could not leap, he could not run,
He could not climb the forest tree.
He knew not *what* to kill; the sun
Scorched him intolerably.

And while he wondered what to do
And how to prove his mighty worth,
Some passer-by's unheeding shoe
Trampled him into earth.

FOR A DEAD KITTEN

Put the rubber mouse away,
Pick the spools up from the floor.
What was velvet-shod, and gay,
Will not want them, any more—

What was warm, is strangely cold.
Where dissolved the little breath?
How could this small body hold
So immense a thing as Death?

THE MONKEY

They strove to rouse him to a rage
By thumping at the bars,
By puffing smoke into his cage
From venomous cigars.

They pelted him with peanut shells
And whacked their noisy hands,
They bellowed raucous syllables
No monkey understands.

The while he sat, grotesque, unkempt,
Devoid of any grace,
But with an infinite contempt
Upon his narrow face.

WORDS FOR A YOUNG WILD THING

Beware
The soundless wing blurring across the moon,
And in the day's blue noon
The slanted wing slicing the bright air.

Take care
So lightly, warily to go, that if
You hear the least twig snap, you can be off
Before the small sound die upon the ear.

Consider how
Plausibly the smooth grass conceals the snare,
How Death slips from his lair
To lie along the bough.

Leaf's turn, year's turn,
In a dry season or the spring at flood,
Whatever stalks your world is out for blood.
See to it that you learn.

TIDAL POOL

Here, at the turning of the tide,
The sea swung in against the shore,
And drew a long, slow breath, and tried
Again, and gained a cranny more.

Its fingers probed the ledges, bare,
Dry in the alien sun, and then
Withdrew, but the small creatures there
Under the kelp took heart again.

Feeling their element flow back
The little worlds of pools became
Suddenly animate; the slack
Ribbons of weed rose up like flame

And wavered on the watery floor.
The mussel, from his pearly house
Peered out; the snail unlatched his door,
Righted himself, began to browse

Along his pasturage of rock.
The shrimp, in arched and flimsy mail
Went skittering backwards, and a flock
Of spiders skated, under sail.

I, leaning from my point of air,
Could almost, by a sleight of mind,
Become a size with them, and share
A world, a universe, defined

By smaller boundaries, but which bore
Like mine, such purpose and such pride,
As if they both were something more
Than a brief interval of tide.

ON FINDING A SNAKE,
WITH ITS HEAD CRUSHED

If I had been the one you met
On this most inauspicious day,
I should have stepped aside, and let
You go upon your way.

Heeding your quiet, courteous hiss,
I should have said, with quick-caught breath,
"Peace to you, neighbor. Isn't this
Too good an hour for Death?"

I should have known that life must be
(Lord of this warm and rocky shelf)
Not relatively more to me
Than to your narrow self,

And, feeling thus, have gone away
And left you, with no lack of speed.
This is too gay and glad a day
For anything to bleed.

INCIDENT IN GETHSEMANE

I am the snake in Eden cursed
For that old mischief with the Tree.
And in this grove, Gethsemane,
A quiet garden, like the first,
I coiled myself upon a stone,
Waiting to see what I should see.
I saw a young man, all alone,
Who knelt and cried upon God's name,
Stifling his moan, as a man must.
And out of pity for Your son
(Though of *Your* pity I had none)
Creeping upon my belly I came
And with my flickering tongue I kissed
His naked heel, and, harmless, laid
On his worn sandal, in the dust,
My unregenerate, dangerous head.

Remember it, Mine Enemy!

IN THE GARDEN

I

The Lizard

What suddenly brought the gray moths out
To dance and flutter everywhere?
Some breath of evening before evening?
Some cool and subtle shift of air?
The lizard knows. He is aware.
Whatever signaled life and flight
Notified Death; and when they light
The lizard will be waiting there.

II

Local Bethesda

Though to this pool descend
No Seraph from on high
With heavenly alchemy
To solace and to mend,
I count it no mean thing
That, rank upon feathered rank,
There stoop to this small brink
Bright visitors from the sky,
That these waters be stirred
For my soul's comforting
If by no angel's wing,
By that of a kind bird.

". . . Wars and rumors of wars. . . ."

Does nothing live at peace?
Nothing, nothing at all,
No matter how weak, how small?
Endless hostilities
Enlist the birds; the mice
Quarrel in the crumbling wall.

The lizard has defined
A square of sunny stone
As his, and from his own
Drives off his kin and kind.
The blind mole meets the blind,
And hates him to the bone.

The narrowest breast extant
Has room enough for rage.
On airy pilgrimage
Flies touch, and take affront.
The gnat's on murder bent,
Great wars the ants engage.

A native anger spurs
The tiniest claw and sting.
And how shall we, who bring
Our own essential curse
The ancient rule reverse
Into some better thing?

Yet stubborn in the face
Of universal strife,
Half beast, half God, his life
Compound of greed and grace,
Stands man, with a drawn knife,
And dares to dream of peace!

Under the Arbor

Mrs. Arachnid,
Plump, domestic,
Steps from her doorsill,
Peers at the day;
Mends a curtain
With new elastic,
Wraps up a parcel,
Puts it away.

Mrs. Arachnid
And I, a woman,
Observe each other
Keeping house,
And each perceives
That, altogether,
We've much in common,
The two of us.

Each, a housewife,
Rests from her labors,
Each of us sitting
Under the vine;
Not quite friends,
But courteous neighbors,
She tends to *her* knitting,
And I to mine.

SANCTUARY

Come, fur and feather—
You with the heart-shaped hooves, the ankles of fine steel,
Death's at your heel;
And into the covert, you doves, murmuring together!

Quick, paw and pinion—
You with the robber mask like a Halloween child;
You with the brown breast, the speckled breast, you with
    the mild
Habit and voice—quick, into the canyon!

Plume-tail, tuft-tail,
Into the thicket with you, quick, under the hedge—
And you with the dragging brush, crouch by the ledge.
Perhaps it will avail—

But he was not to be denied.
Death entered with you, he would not be bereft.
Here in the dust, ripped from his ensign, he left
A soiled ribbon of blood, that wrinkled as it dried.

THE BEASTS

"*. . . and the beasts of the field shall be at peace with thee.*"

JOB 5: 23

Oh think—the satin-skinned, the dappled,
The doe with her fawn
Standing at gaze, calm-eyed, untroubled,
Their terror gone.

Think—the round rabbit, the plumed squirrel,
The lynx, too,
And the wolf, forgetful of his quarrel
With man, with you.

Even the curved panther, he
With knives along his jaw—
How soft that heavy head upon your knee,
And his furled paw!

INCIDENT WITH LIONS

Into the Ark, by docile two and seven,
The obedient animals filed.
But there were some, I think, too proud, too wild
Thus to be herded and driven.
Lions, surely, who shook the night with thunder
There on the last hill,
Drenched and bedraggled and doomed, but imperial still,
Watching the world go under.
Noah had trouble finding some of that kin
Whom he could hustle aboard.
At bay, the princely lions paced and roared
And would not save their skin.
They stood while the heavens split and the Flood rolled
And chose to drown deep
To the company of jackal and rat and the witless sheep
In the Ark's stinking hold.

THE BEASTS AT JUDGMENT

"And he was there in the wilderness forty days,
tempted of Satan; and was with the wild beasts."

MARK 1: 13

We are the friendly beasts,
We knew this Jesus well.
Full forty days and nights
The Lord with us did dwell.

Lean limb and padded paw
We followed in His track;
And not a claw unsheathed,
And not a lip writhed back.

We watched with gentle eyes
When down He laid Him,
No jackal in the land
Would have betrayed Him!

Our tongues had licked the dust
From His worn sandal;
We brought our round-eyed young
For Him to fondle.

Lion and leopard and wolf—
We would have ministered to Him.
We were the friendly beasts.
His own kind slew Him.

"SURELY I WOULD SPEAK TO THE
ALMIGHTY, AND I DESIRE TO
REASON WITH GOD."

JOB 13: 3

ON CONTEMPLATING AN HONEST,
ROSY-CHEEKED APPLE

Why it should suit
God's pleasure, at Creation,
To make this decent fruit
The symbol of temptation,

Has always seemed to me
A curious deflection
From the more general harmony
Of His selection.

In Eden, were there not
Glamorous fruits growing?
Pomegranate, tangerine, apricot,
Grapes, darkly glowing?

After all's said and done,
For purpose so destructive,
Could He have chosen one
Less wantonly seductive!

ONE HESITANT

". . . *but we shall all be changed, in a moment, in the twinkling of an eye, at the last trump.*"

I CORINTHIANS 15: 52

But this known body, this familiar shell,
Follows the angles of my soul so well!
Having been worn thus long and comfortably,
It has become too integrally *me*.

I am afraid that on that Final Day,
Stripped of its threadbare but beloved clay,
And stared at by a radiant angel band,
Self-conscious and abashed my soul will stand

Wanting again the shabby flesh it had,
So stiff and strange, in its white raiment clad!

TEXT

Because I heard His ways were just,
In God's strong hand I placed my trust.

I saw a child born lame and blind;
I saw a man of honest mind
In his own house despoiled and slain
By thieves who lived to spoil again.

I saw a woman's honor sold
By her own lovely hand, for gold.
She flourished to her life's soft close,
While homely virtue starved and froze.

I saw the meek, accepting dearth,
Fall heir to some six feet of earth,
But arrogance did not hesitate
To claim the whole of man's estate.

Charity furrowed his dry plain,
While on greed's acres fell God's rain.
Truth withered in a rocky cleft
With bay trees blossoming right and left.

I saw how red the rivers ran
Where man struck down his brother man.
Ten million murders brought to pass
All by the jawbone of an ass.

I found another verse, which read
More to my credence, for it said
Briefly, with less to rearrange
For faith's sad eyes: "His ways are strange . . ."

THE FIRE

I like the building of an open fire
But for one feature:
Inevitably, as the flame licks higher
Wrapping the logs, there scuttles from a crack
Some minute but distinguishable creature
Smoked from his room,
Who halts, appalled; sniffs doom,
Ducks hastily back,
Is driven forth, runs, desperate, that way and this,
Is blocked by an abyss,
Stops, wavering, in his track,
Falls, struggles, shrivels, dies,
Before my eyes.

This harrowing spectacle *I* cannot view
Unwrenched by pity. Though, if accounts be true,
A like reaction, at a Later Day,
Should not be expected, Father in Heaven, of You.

THE FAVORED

O bless His Holy Name, indeed.
Thank Him, though half a world may bleed,
Your loves still live, your walls still stand,
He holds you in His hollowed hand.

O bless His Holy Name, rejoice.
He singled out your little voice
And heard and heeded when you cried,
Although a thousand others died.

Come, thank Him on your bended knees
That you were numbered not with these
Who called on Him with equal trust
And got for answer blood and dust.

Ten thousand at your right hand fell—
But you are safe, and warm, and well
According to His loving plan.
O pray and praise Him, if you can!

THESE HANDS

"In the image of God created he him . . ."
GENESIS 1: 27

These hands are shaped like God's, and so
Let them be careful what they do.

Let them be quick to lift the weak,
Let them be kind as they are strong,
Let them defend the silent meek
Against the many-languaged wrong.

These hands are shaped like God's. Be sure
They bear the mark of no man's pain
Who asked their help to make secure
His little roof—and asked in vain.

These hands are shaped like God's. Take care
They catch the sparrow hurled from air.

Lest God look down from Heaven, and see
What things are wrought beneath the sun
By us, His images, and be
Ashamed of what His hands have done.

ACCUSATION

*". . . what man is there of you, whom if his son
ask bread, will he give him a stone?"*

MATTHEW 7: 9

But this man starved before he died,
For all Your word assures.
Did You not hear him when he cried?
Was he no child of Yours?

Where were You, yesterday,
That hour his eyes grew dim,
Turning Your cloudy face away,
Stretching no hand to him!

IN FLOOD AND DEARTH

"People went to church in rowboats. . . ."

NEWSPAPER CLIPPING

Such has His kindness been to me
That I His name could bless
And fall upon my bended knee
In simple selfishness,

But that I see in flood and dearth
How harsh His hand doth lie
Throughout the length and breadth of earth
On better folk than I.

A taint of Reason in the skull,
It is a perilous thing
For such blind faith as any fool
Might hold his comforting—

For if, in truth, His purposed power
Has sent the storm abroad,
Then am I humbled most before
Man's charity to God.

Oh it must shame Him to His face,
If, out of Heaven, He notes
The feeble, gasping squeak of praise
From the surviving throats.

JACOB SINGS

Better than valleys, and the narrow grace
Of willows leaning to the river's face,
The terrible, male beauty of this place.

Better than vineyards is the brawny sand,
And the stout breathing of this lusty land,
Wind in the ears, and the sky on either hand!

I have abjured the subtle-bosomed south,
And the soft rains, like honey on the mouth.
Here is a muscled fasting, and a drouth.

For I have found the grape too sickly sweet,
And I am wearied of the docile wheat—
But here, if one be strong enough, is meat!

A brave life, Israel, for the spirit grown
Wakeful and fierce—and many a man has known
A harder pillow than an honest stone.

THE HAPPY LAND

"A melodious noise of birds in the spreading
branches, a running that could not be seen of skipping
beasts. All the world shined with clear light,
and none was hindered in his labor."

APOCRYPHA

Where is that happy land, oh where
In what far country of the mind?
And may one rise and journey there
And dwell among this pleasant kind?
Say, would the wayworn wanderer find
Freedom and peace and balm for care
In such a golden light as shined
On Eden, through an earlier air?

Oh might he build a little house
With his own hands, and turn the sod,
Unhindered work, and play, and feast—
Friends with himself, and with his God,
With them that sing among the boughs,
And every soft-eyed, skipping beast?

THE FIGHT

*"O Death, how bitter is the remembrance of thee
to a man who is at peace with his possessions . . ."*
APOCRYPHA

But not to him alone
Whose happy breath is drawn
In peace amid his lands,
With plenty in his hands
And all that makes breath good,
The thought of Death is bad.

To him, as well, whose life
Is anguished and unsafe,
And whose possessions' scope
Is nothing but his hope,
The face of Death is still
Most to be shunned, and vile.

For even if he cry
In his extremest day
"Sweet Death . . ." He lies! He lies!
Himself that speech denies.
His every part shall strive
To keep that man alive.

His will gives no assent
To the supreme affront;
He clings with desperate strength
To living's breadth and length.
And when the will has done,
The stubborn flesh fights on.

173

"AS IT WAS IN THE BEGINNING . . ."

The Brotherhood of Man, I know.
There were two brothers, long ago;
And there was precedent begun:
The stronger slew the weaker one.

WITNESS FOR THE DEFENSE

WITNESS FOR THE DEFENSE

I am the Elder Brother, and that one
Who, having borne all day the heat of the sun,
Begrudged the equal penny given a neighbor
For his eleventh-hour labor.
Among that provident company am I
Whose lamps were burning high,
Who clustered in about the Wedding Table
With time and oil to spare. And, in the fable,
I am that thrifty spinster, the Rich Ant
Who told the mendicant
Grasshopper to go and dance the winter through.
And I am Martha, too,
Bustling about the kitchen and the dairy,
Complaining to my Friend, nagging at Mary.

Self-righteous, petty, stingy and unkind,
All these am I, grasping and mean of mind,
And these unlovely attributes serve well
As posts whereon to pin the parable.
While I see to it that the fields are tilled,
The harvest gathered in, the granary filled,
The vineyard planted and the hearthstone swept,
The tithes and taxes paid, the farmstead kept.

EDEN

I

"And the Lord God planted a garden eastward in Eden . . ."
GENESIS 2: 8

Behold the treacherous garden, long ago,
With the first April candidly abroad,
When docile leopard fed with trustful doe,
And Eve talked nightly with a friendly God.
Behold the happy beasts—and one who was
More subtil than the rest; the spotted guise
Of Death coiled lightly in the innocent grass
Watching the woman with his lidless eyes.

Consider Eden, in those first gold days,
Sunny and green and loud with bird and bee,
How God walked softly down the murmurous ways—
And the Snake throve, and the disastrous Tree
Put forth its ominous freight of leaf and bud,
That Eve's dark son might shed his brother's blood.

II

"Now the serpent was more subtil than any beast
of the field which the Lord God had made."
GENESIS 3: 1

"Ye shall become as Gods," the serpent said.
And God was zealous in His own behalf.
Wherefore He smote the heavens with His staff,
And the stars splintered and the planets fled,
And Eden trembled, and the leopards ran
Snarling into the alleys of the grass,
And mountains split to let the Lord God pass,
Seeking the terrified transgressor, man.

Pity the two who cowered, cheek to cheek,
Pity the disobedient pair who lay
Frightened and sick with shame, and cold as clay.
How could they answer God? How could they speak?
Pity whatever poor defense they made,
Cheated by Satan, and to God betrayed.

III

"*And when the woman saw that the tree was good*
for food, and that it was pleasant to the eyes,
and a tree to be desired to make one wise,
she took of the fruit thereof . . ."

GENESIS 3: 6

Eve speaks:
Herein the crafty serpent tempted me:
He said "Ye shall be wise as God is wise.
Subtler than God intended man to be."
Wherefore I ate, and bartered Paradise.
Not for *myself*, mind you, but for my lord
Adam, who also looked upon the Tree,
I braved the angel, and despised the sword,
And was desirous of a God's degree.

And here lies all the measure of my blame:
That one for whom I dreamed so proud a span
Fell short the very stature of a man,
And would not even own our common shame;
But mumbled, cringing at Jehovah's feet,
"The woman tempted me, and I did eat."

IV

*"And the man said, The woman whom thou gavest
to be with me, she gave me of the tree . . ."*

GENESIS 3: 12

Adam speaks:
Surely, I thought, that God Who stooped to dust
And fashioned me of earth, and of my flesh
Wrought the disturbing miracle afresh,
Surely that God is generous, as just.
Seeing He set the serpent in her path
(She who was flower and flint, and fragile air,
Gentle and willful and withal most fair)
Might He not, so perceiving, stay His wrath?

Therefore I laid to Eve the first offense,
Hoping, as well, Jehovah might recall
How He had made her lovelier than all
Wisdom or caution or obedience.
Which futile and most desperate device
She labeled villainy and cowardice!

V

"And the woman conceived, and bare Cain . . ."

GENESIS 4: 1

Consider now old Eden's tainted shoot,
That firstborn son, the child who must have been
Sprung from the festered bitterness between
The woman and the man; the evil fruit
Became the dark inheritance of Cain,
Poor warped, rejected, sullen demi-brute
With all the venom of that old dispute
Gall in his throat, and poison in his brain.

Conceived in anguish, and in terror born,
Drinking resentment from a flowing breast,
What fault of his, whose graceless flesh possessed
His father's fury, and his mother's scorn?
So shaped in enmity before his birth,
Small wonder that he struck his kin to earth!

SIC TRANSIT

The Cities of the Plain are dust;
Assyria is fox's plunder;
Sidon and Tyre to silence thrust,
Nineveh fallen, with fire and thunder.
Across the margin of the world
The drift of Babylon is swirled,
And centuries of rot and rust
Have gnawed Capernaum asunder.

Stone crumbles—but more staunchly fares
A dust incredibly translated:
Judas still haggles at his wares,
Cain is forever new-created.
Delilah, in a Paris frock,
Goes out to tea at five o'clock.
Salome climbs the Subway stairs,
Potiphar takes the Elevated.

THE PRODIGAL

They made a feast in the banquet hall,
And the calf was slain for the prodigal.
And here I sit, while the last guests linger,
With a robe on my back, and a ring on my finger.

Well, home calls somehow, the whole world through,
And its threshold portal is a dream come true,
And the glow of the home hearth is beautiful to see
When one has been a vagrant, in a Far Country.

Oh it's not much fun to be swine herd keeping,
And to bed with the hard earth is cold enough sleeping,
And after the husks were gone, I fasted—
But Oh my friends—while the money lasted!

THE FATHER

Well, he's come home, this younger son of mine.
But something in his penitence betrays
He had been guardian of fouler swine,
Before those latter days. . . .

For there's a furtive something sliding under
His speech; he sits and twists his ring around
And stares at it. My son was lost—I wonder,
Is he so truly found?

Oh I am glad I did not hesitate
To run and clasp him hard in my embrace.
Still, it was rather more than fortunate
He could not see *my* face.

THE ELDER SON

*"I say unto you, that likewise joy shall be in heaven
over one sinner that repenteth, more than over ninety
and nine just persons, which need no repentance."*

LUKE 15: 7

What profit hath the Elder Son,
Toiling amid his father's walls,
If, since the world was first begun,
Feasts have been laid for prodigals

Who put away their threadbare sin
And stagger home, repentance voicing?
Even the angels hail them in
With what a ratio of rejoicing!

FOR LOT'S WIFE

Maybe there were curtains blowing at the casement,
Maybe in the garden little leaves and new,
Jars and jars of spice in a moss-cool basement,
Maybe at the doorsill a bright flower blew . . .

Lintel and threshold and a hearth fire burning—
God, that for this tending fashioned womankind,
If You bade her leave them, and never be returning,
How could You expect her not to look behind?

DELILAH

They bound, and took him south,
A year ago—and yet
I cannot quite forget
His kiss upon my mouth,

Nor his dark head that lay
Night long upon my breast.
Samson, I had not guessed
All that I might betray.

Oh he was straight of limb,
Goodly to look upon—
Humbled, in Gaza's town,
What have they done to him . . . !

By day he walks in might
The chambers of my mind;
Shackled, and maimed, and blind
He comes to me by night.

BEHOLD THIS DREAMER

"And Joseph dreamed a dream, and he told it his
brethren: and they hated him yet the more."

GENESIS 37: 5

I tell you, they liked me not, from the very beginning.
They were banded together against me, eleven to one,
Although I was guileless enough, and the youngest son,
And only given to dreams, and the reckless spinning
Of arrogant visions whose telling had little savor
For those I prophesied would bow down before me.
But my father reckoned the pitiful hurt that tore me,
And gave me a princely robe, and his old-man's favor.

I was overly proud of my colorful coat, it seems,
And lacked the natural wit, or the tact, to hide it,
For my brothers' raiment was shabby and dull, beside it.
Moreover, I prated too often of one of my dreams,
And my envious brethren, liking the tale no whit,
Sold me a slave to Egypt, because of it.

THE NIGHTMARE

"... and Abraham ... bound Isaac his son, and laid him
on the altar ... and took the knife to slay his son."
GENESIS 22: 9–10

He wakens, strangling in his tears,
Again, poor child, I hear him scream
And cannot go to calm his fears.
I am the reason for the dream.

Mine is the nightmare step, the voice,
And mine the nightmare hands that swim
Out of the blackness toward his face—
I am the one who corners him.

He brought me flowers in his fists
To deck the altar I had made.
Even when I bound his childish wrists
He thought it was a game we played!

Oh never in his little life
Had he met fear in any guise—
He looked upon a naked knife;
He read my purpose in my eyes.

Weeping, he wakes. His mother goes
To comfort him. I make no sign.
He trembles if I come too close,
He will not trust his hand to mine.

NOAH

Noah, the righteous man of God,
Hurried his household to the Ark,
And watched the trees begin to bow
And watched the lowering sky grow dark.

He saw the driving ranks of rain
Batter the fields where he had toiled;
He saw his springing wheat go down,
His tender vineyards stripped and spoiled.

He heard the lash of lightning crack
Above the world; he heard the thunder
Loud in the mountains, and he saw
The valleys and the plains go under.

He saw the fertile hillside heave
And crumble with a roaring sound,
And where his blossoming orchard stood
A steaming fissure in the ground.

He saw the pasture turn a lake,
He saw the wooded hollows fill
And inch by inch the creeping tide
Rise from the valley to the hill.

He saw his barns begin to lean,
He heard, above the shrieking wind,
The bawling of his frantic beasts
Tied in their stalls and left behind.

And he could look no more, but still
He looked, and saw the swirling brown
Relentless water reach his house,
And the walls buckle, and go down.

And Noah raised his knotted fists
And shook them at the streaming sky,
Then ground them hard against his mouth
To keep himself from blasphemy.

THE RETURN

Was it worth so much to me, then, to be warmed, to be fed?
I do not remember now how it feels to be cold,
Nor to hunger for more than this meat and these dates and this
    bread
By my father doled.

I was headstrong and willful and foolish; they all knew it.
But have I forgotten how kindly I was met?
Not for a moment. Indeed, my brother sees to it
That I do not forget.

I am clipped and fat and tame as a barnyard fowl.
Was it this that I wanted, there in the swineherd's shack?
Well, I made my choice—but I know, in my heart, in my soul,
I should never have come back!

SWEET STORY OF OLD

"I think, when I read that sweet story of old
When Jesus was here among men . . ."

SUNDAY SCHOOL HYMN

JOSEPH TO MARY

Mary, beloved, if I wounded you
With clumsy silence, or with tardy speech,
It was because my heart was slow to reach
Beyond the limits of its mortal view.
Not that I doubted you, or loved you less,
But it was hard to face the winking town,
And a man's pride is difficult to down,
Whatever faith he may, in truth, profess.

How many nights I watched you, as you lay
With this, the Holy Child, upon your breast;
What tumult shook my heart from day to day—
Oh little Mary, have you never guessed
That I, who would have died to spare you harm,
So feared to clasp you with an earthly arm?

MARY TO JOSEPH

This dread has been upon me, chilled and numbing,
This fear has sat within me from the start,
Since first I told you of the angel's coming
And of the Child that lay beneath my heart.

It was no easy thing to understand
And not by word or deed have you reproved me—
But Joseph, Joseph—when you took my hand,
Did you *believe* me, even as you loved me?

WHEN MARY WAS A LITTLE MAID

When Mary was a little maid,
After the evening touched the hill,
She used to put her candle out
And lean her elbows on the sill
And watch the starry cavalcade—
When Mary was a little maid.

Ah, little Mary, innocent-eyed,
I wonder if you ever knew
A stirring pain, presentiment
Of what those stars would bring to you,
Or clasped your hands, or vaguely sighed—
Ah, little Mary, innocent-eyed.

For those same quiet stars looked down
Upon a Baby in a stall,
Upon a Toddler by your knee,
Upon a Boy so quickly tall,
Upon a certain bloody crown
And cross, outside a jeering town—
And those same quiet stars looked down.

THE GIFTS

"But Mary kept all these things,
and pondered them in her heart."
LUKE 2: 19

So Mary put the gifts away,
But the strange words she kept,
And wakeful many a night she lay
While goodman Joseph slept.

"Frankincense for a king . . ." she thought,
"A crown for a king's head . . .
Was ever such rich treasure brought
Down to a manger bed?"

And once she clasped the Child to her
And kissed His narrow feet,
Remembering the subtle myrrh
That scents a winding sheet.

CHRISTMAS THE YEAR ONE, A.D.

That year no wondering shepherds came,
Nor ever any more
The Magi from the glamorous East
Crowding the narrow door.

There were no gifts of myrrh, or gold,
Or jewels in glittering strands
Too heavy for a child to hold,
Too harsh for baby hands.

But Martha baked a barley cake,
Dorcas a spicy bun,
And goodman Joseph carved a toy
For Mary's little Son.

Timothy brought a woolly lamb,
Esther a fluted shell,
And all day long came friendly folk
To wish young Jesus well.

There was no sudden clash of steel
To make sweet Mary start,
Nor any dark, ambiguous words
Coiling about her heart,

Only the things of home, and peace,
With the calm stars above,
And little Jesus safe among
The holier gifts of love.

MARY

That day the small Christ hurt his hand
Upon a rusty nail,
Joseph could never understand
Why Mary grew so pale

And why she sat, with drooping head
And eyes gone dark with pain,
Long after he was comforted
And sent to play again—

Or why, long after day was done,
And all the household slept,
She knelt beside her little Son
And clasped her hands, and wept.

IN NAZARETH

Our son, who spoke so bravely in the temple
To the wise doctors and the learned men
Came home with us. In Nazareth again
He and my Joseph went about the simple
Business of carpentry, and he grew stronger
And taller day by day, and the years flew—
Such busy, happy years, and ah so few
Till suddenly he was a child no longer.

And I remembered every curious saying,
Watching him, knowing he was set apart
Even from the time he lay beneath my heart.
Sometimes I thought I saw a strange light play
About his head, and felt my heart grow cold
Seeing him heave an oak beam to his shoulder.

THE CHILD

"And Jesus called a little child unto him,
and set him in the midst of them . . ."
MATTHEW 18: 2

Though it was long ago
And I so young and small,
As it were yesterday
So clear can I recall

His face, his speaking eyes,
And how he stooped to me
And took me in his arms
And set me on his knee.

I knew, as children know,
That he was kind and good,
And that he was my friend,
Although I understood

Not half of what he said
About his father's home,
Where those of childlike heart
And childlike faith should come.

But I remember well
His gentle voice, the way
He smiled—and how I wept
When I was led away!

IN THE SERVANTS' HALL

*". . . And Peter followed afar off. And when they had kindled a fire
in the midst of the hall, and were set down together, Peter sat down
among them. But a certain maid beheld him as he sat by the fire,
and earnestly looked upon him, and said, This man was also with
him. And he denied him, saying, Woman, I know him not."*

LUKE 22: 54–57

When first he answered me, I knew he lied.
The cloak about his shame was much too thin
To hide it from a woman's eyes. Beside,
I saw him, when they brought the prisoner in

Following afar off. And yet to seek
Another proof, I looked at him and said
"This man was also with him. Let him speak
And he betrays himself." He shook his head

And turned away. By nature being perverse
For very spite I asked again. Alack,
The fellow turned on me with such a curse
That even I, a kitchen wench, fell back.

They left at cock-crow. *That* for such as he!
But of the man whom he denied as friend,
One thing I know—had he so looked at me,
I would have followed him, to the world's end . . .

NIGHT OF CALVARY

*". . . and the earth did quake, and the rocks rent;
and the graves were opened. . . ."*

Suddenly, on the shaken earth
Thick darkness dropped like lead,
And startled sepulchers cast forth
The rude-awakened dead.

Shuddering from the graves they came,
Stumbling on fleshless feet,
Each clasping to his shrunken frame
His moldy winding sheet.

They clicked across the shivering plain,
They crowded here and there,
Frightened to find themselves again
In the forgotten air.

Across the blackened world they fled
Through mire and field and fell,
The pitiful, bewildered dead,
Looking for Gabriel.

And when the livid light returned
Each where his grave had been
Stood whimpering in the chill, and yearned
To lay him down therein.

Each, fumbling, stretched his narrow girth
On the unfeeling stones,
Till by and by the kindly earth
Sheltered the timid bones,

Covered them from the impious day
And closed each hollow eye.
But taut and terrified they lay,
Palpitant still they lie,

They quiver at the roar of rain,
Wakeful in dust they cower—
How could they ever sleep again,
Remembering that Hour?

THE NEIGHBORS

*"And he . . . came into his own country . . . and when the sabbath
day was come, he began to teach. . . . and many hearing him were
astonished, saying, From whence hath this man these things? . . . Is
not this the carpenter, the son of Mary, the brother of James, and
Joses, and of Juda, and Simon? and are not his sisters here with us?
And they were offended at him.*

*But Jesus said unto them, A prophet is not without honour, but in
his own country, and among his own kin, and in his own house."*

MARK 6: 1–4

News of the trouble in Jerusalem,
His trial, and the manner of his death,
Came to his own village, and to his neighbors,
The people of Nazareth.

They talked. "His mother'll take it pretty hard.
She set great store by him—though I must say
He treated her, at least to *my* way of thinking,
In a mighty high-handed way."

"Why, you remember the time, he was just a boy,
He give them such a scare?
Lost himself three days in Jerusalem
And never turned a hair

When they found him, but answered back, as cool as you please,
He was doing his father's business, or some such truck,
As if most of us hadn't known his father, Joseph,
Since he was knee high to a duck.

And *his* business was carpentry, not talking back to priests!"
"But Mary, she always remembered it. Some claim
She was a little bit touched—had visions and all—
Before he came."

"She was always partial to him, but if you ask *me*
He'd a been a better son
If he'd stayed home and raised a family
Like his brothers done."

"The trouble with him, he didn't use his judgment.
He was forever speaking out,
Though many's the time I've told him: there's *some* wrong things
Folks just don't talk about."

"They say, though, in some parts of the country
He drew quite a crowd. Five thousand or more. I don't know—
Here in Nazareth nobody'd walk two blocks to hear him,
And it probably ain't so."

"It's hard on his family, the disgrace and all.
And I'm sorry about him. I was his friend.
I liked him, you understand. But I always said
He'd come to a bad end."

BALLAD OF THE GOLDEN BOWL

"What is this golden bowl, mother,
With its strange design?
It is not like our other things,
But foreign, and fine . . ."

"It came out of the East, child,
A long time ago.
Your grandmother gave it to us.
This is all we know:

When your father's brother was born
On a winter's night,
A new star stood in the skies—
It was a great sight!

And three kings rode from afar
To kneel at his bed.
They were seeking a greater King,
Or so they said . . ."

"And was he a King, mother,
My father's kin?"
"No, child. It was all a mistake.
It must have been . . .

For they went away, those three,
And they came no more.
And he had a sad life, child,
He died poor . . ."

"Had he a wife, mother,
And a boy of his own?"
"He had neither chick nor child, darling,
He was all alone.

He was a good man,
But he came to grief,
And they hanged him on a cross
Like a common thief."

"But why, mother, why?
If he was kind and good?"
"It was a plot of some sort, child,
We never understood.

There was nothing we could do,
Being humble folk.
He was your grandmother's favorite.
Her heart broke.

She gave us this golden bowl
When she came to die.
It is sad—it is all we have
To remember him by. . . ."

THE SEARCH

"Yet dearly do I love Thee, and would be loved fain . . ."

JOHN DONNE

ULTIMATE VALOR

The mind is very brave, God knows.
Erect and unafraid it goes
From dark to dark, and staunch, essays
The cruelest and most tortuous ways.

Yet lacks, withal, a final grace,
Whatever perils it may face,
Because so great a fear it hath
Of faith's incalculable path.

THE SEARCH

I sought Him where my logic led.
"This friend is always sure and right.
His lamp will give sufficient light.
I need no Star," I said.

I sought Him in the city square,
Logic and I went up and down
The marketplace of many a town,
But He was never there.

I tracked Him to the mind's far rim;
The clever intellect went forth
To east and west and south and north
But found no trace of Him.

We walked the world from sun to sun,
Logic and I, and Little Faith,
But never came to Nazareth,
Nor met the Holy One.

We sought in vain. And finally
Back to the heart's small house I crept
And fell upon my knees, and wept.
And Lo! He came to me!

DE PROFUNDIS

Lord, I have lost my way, who was so sure.
My candle gutters to a glimmering spark—
I cannot long endure
The terror, and the dark.

Father, my plumes are bowed;
My arrogant sword is shattered, hilt and blade.
I am no longer proud,
I am afraid.

Wilt Thou forgive the pride,
The foolish mockery I flung at Thee,
And let me come, as children do, and hide
My face against Thy knee?

Wilt Thou forget the passion, and the pain,
Give back the simple heart whose faith sufficed,
That questioned not? And let me find again
My brother, Christ?

DEFENSE

". . . if thou doest not well, sin lieth at the door."
GENESIS 4: 7

In whatever guise you wear,
Trouble me no more.
Naked flesh, or scale, or hair,
Quit my door!

Do you speak, or hiss, or whine,
Double tongue or one,
You shall force no sill of mine—
Get you gone!

Though he stand, or coil, or crouch,
Surely Satan sees
I am safe beside my couch,
On my knees.

BESIDE THE BROOK

I read it in the Holy Book:
Just such a smooth and polished stone
Young David gathered from the brook,
And with a shepherd's sling alone
The Man of Gath was overthrown.

Now, in the current of my mind,
I plunge an eager hand, and pray
That by some magic I may find
The certain stone to suit my need:
An apt and neatly rounded creed,
A deadly, smooth philosophy
Wherewith to arm myself, and slay
The Philistine confronting me.

PRAYER TO MARY

Holy Mary, God's Mother,
Wilt thou look from heaven?
Thou who wast a woman, too,
Grant that I be given
Such sweet measure of thy grace,
Such white strength of thee
As my slender soul may wear
Well, and fittingly.
Walk with me these troubled days,
Till the dark be past,
That I need not drop my gaze
Meeting thine, at last.

"NOT MADE WITH HANDS . . ."

I shall build up my house anew,
With sturdier roof and walls and floor,
A fairer dwelling, and more true
Than served the soul before.

It was a shining place enough,
But God is an observant guest,
And every flaw in shoddy stuff
Were straightway manifest.

The timbers of a selfish heart
Will crumble at the wind's assault,
By no apology nor art
Could I defend the fault.

This masonry of little worth,
These walls unfit for His degree,
The cheap Penates on my hearth,
I cannot let Him see. . . .

Christ was a goodly carpenter,
His honest eye would pierce me through
With greater shame than I could bear—
I build my house anew.

"THEREFORE WITH ANGELS AND ARCHANGELS...."

". . . Therefore with Angels and Archangels
and with all the company of Heaven,
we laud and magnify Thy glorious name. . . ."
BOOK OF COMMON PRAYER

Lord, Thou art kind, indeed,
To such as cry to Thee,
Permitting them to enter in
This goodly Company,

But Oh more gracious far,
That Thou dost not disown
The smallest, rapt-eyed, trembling soul
Speechless, before Thy throne.

H